S

BOY

THE MYSTICAL BODY

BY THE SAME AUTHOR.

THIS TREMENDOUS LOVER.
A MYSTIC UNDER ARMS.
DIFFICULTIES IN MENTAL PRAYER.

THE MYSTICAL BODY

THE FOUNDATION OF THE SPIRITUAL LIFE

BY

FATHER M. EUGENE BOYLAN, O.Cist.R.

THE NEWMAN BOOKSHOP
Westminster, Maryland
1948

Cum permissu Superiorum

Nihil Obstat:

  JACOBUS BASTIBLE, S.T.D.,
    Censor Deputatus.

Imprimatur:

  ✠ DANIEL,
    Episcopus Corcagiensis.
7 Januarii, 1947.

TO
MARY
THE MOTHER OF
THE WHOLE CHRIST
AND
TO THE MOTHER
WHO GAVE ME LIFE

CONTENTS

INTRODUCTION*

A RECALL TO THE SPIRITUAL LIFE

THE Mercier Press declared, from the moment of its inception, that its program is one in which religion is the vital influence. No secret was made of the fact that it regards itself as an organ of Christian wisdom, the illumination of which is faith. In this light The Mercier Press accepts the Church of God on earth, the Catholic Church, and, like the great cardinal to whom it owes its inspiration, it has no other ambition than to share with men of good will the secrets of divine wisdom. On one occasion Mercier addressed an audience in these words: "It may happen that amongst you there are individuals who do not share my faith; but I see no reason why I should excuse its presence in everything I say." Any other attitude would have been incompatible with the character of a man whose sincerity was indisputable and who was too enlightened not to realize that the secret of power, in literature as in life, is the living force of true conviction.

The Catholic Church is the mystical Body of Jesus Christ, by means of which He lives again in the world of time and space. "For it is indeed Christ," writes the present Holy Father, Pius XII, "who lives in the Church, and through her teaches, governs, and sancti-

*From the Irish edition.

fies." It follows that the life and action of the Church is the continued action of Jesus, with whom the Church forms one mystic Person. Now the principal action of Jesus, Priest and Saviour, is that of sanctification. And since sanctity, in His intentions, is nothing less than a sharing in the life of the Godhead, the primary rôle of the Church on earth is that of being, for men, the source of eternal life. It would be false to infer that the Church is indifferent to the things of time or to the natural needs of men. To think so would be not only to misconceive the notion of eternal life, the seeds of which must be sown in time, but to forget the character of Jesus, who in the desert took pity on the hunger of the multitude.

Nature, as well as grace, is ultimately from God, and a wondrous harmony reigns between them: grace perfects nature. In this conviction the Church adapts herself to human needs. It is by an appeal to reason, in the first instance, that the Church establishes her claim to a hearing as the appointed teaching authority on the things of God, and it is only when she has brought into captivity the understanding unto the obe-dience of Christ (I Corinthians, x, 5) that she exercises her power of ruling. But the fact remains, and it is a tremendous fact, that the essential mission of the Church on earth is to be the source of eternal life for men; and it is only by life that death, in all its forms, can finally be conquered.

A recall to the spiritual life is nothing less than an

urgent invitation to enter into possession of the more abundant life that Christ, through the medium of His Church, is thirsting to communicate to souls. It is this more abundant life that must vivify the body of religious theory and practice in the present economy. Religion, as a living thing, comprises many elements, but at its source there is, and must be, an attitude of mind and spirit. *But the hour cometh and now is,* said our Blessed Lord at the well of Jacob, *when the true adorers shall adore the Father in spirit and in truth. For the Father also seeketh such to adore him* (*John, iii, 23*). To direct the attention of men to the adoration of God, in spirit and in truth, is to point to the source of living waters where life itself, as well as religion, is concerned.

For many years important initiatives on the part of the Church have been stressing this recall to the spirit-ual life as the one thing necessary for our civilization. With the name of Leo XIII is associated a return to Thomism destined to benefit the intellectual life of re-ligion; Pius X initiated a liturgical movement in which he invited the faithful to a more intimate association in the official worship of the Church; Benedict XV gave important principles for the regulation of life amongst the nations; Pius XI outlined a program of Catholic action that awakened men to the duty of apostolate. But animating these initiatives, and giving them the complete coherence of concerted action, is the reiterated emphasis of each succeeding pontiff on the supernatural character of the life by which the world must be saved for God. Of this emphasis a most impressive example is to be found in the encyclical letter *Mystici Corporis Christi* of July 4, 1943. "The doctrine of the Mystical Body of Christ," writes the Holy Father, "has a surpassing splendor which commends it to the mediation of all who are moved by the divine Spirit, and with the light which it sheds upon their minds, is a powerful stimulus to the salutory conduct which it enjoins."

Inspired by this solicitude of the Church for the eternal interests of the human spirit, The Mercier Press is inaugurating, under the general editorship of Father James, O.F.M.Cap., a series of books dealing with the various aspects of the spiritual life. It is hoped that the series will be entirely Catholic in tone, drawing on various authors for cooperation, and endeavoring to meet the actual needs of our contemporaries. The present age, so rich in many things, is poor in wisdom, and if it be true, as it is, that "not on bread alone doth man live," The Mercier Press feels justified in thinking that, by this recall to the Spiritual Life, it is carrying out its mission.

JOHN M. FEEHAN,
Director,
THE MERCIER PRESS LIMITED
Cork, Eire

PREFACE BY THE GENERAL EDITOR

IT was characteristic of our Blessed Lord to express the most sublime truths in the simplest manner. Truths from another sphere, truths beyond the mind's capacity to discover or understand, He would clothe in the imagery of daily life. That is why His teaching is so filled with the beauty of parable and of figure, ranging from the flight of a bird in the air to the grace of the lily in the field, and why His every sentence is a source of light from heaven. The method was appropriate. Jesus was Himself the great invisible made visible, the eternal Spirit wedded to sense and imagination, and His aim was to draw men from the things that perish into the life-giving mystery of Godhead of which He was, before their eyes, the living sacrament and sign.

On the lips of our Lord parables were intended to communicate the splendor of His own vision; in images accessible to men He gave shape and form to truths invisible to mankind. When He wished to announce the mystery of creative love, He evoked before their eyes the image of a man in the fields scattering seeds in the earth. *Behold the sower went forth to sow* . . . . Nothing could be simpler, more sublime, more profound. Towards the end, allowing the same thought to find a new expression, He said: *Amen, amen I say to you, unless the grain of wheat falling into the ground die, itself remaineth alone. But if it die, it bringeth forth much fruit* . . . . No man could have lived three years with Jesus and imagine that it was His ambition to remain alone. He had called, and gathered, disciples to Him; He was on the point of instituting the sacrament of their union with Him; and He was thinking of the death on the morrow by means of which He would sow the seed of eternal life in the earth of humanity.

It is remarkable how frequently the Master reverts to this image, or similar ones, to bring home the design of God in man's salvation. The explanation is not far to seek. In all the thoughts of our Blessed Lord there was *one* thought, as in His every desire beat the pulse of one supreme desire, and nothing could satisfy the Heart of Him save the reunion of man with God in the intimacy of His own Person. He was about to die, as the seed in the earth dies, but the thought of our Blessed Lord at this moment did not rest in death: He would rise again. He would be, in this world of sin and decay and death, a veritable Tree of Life for all who would accept Him. And because that thought was deep in the mind of the Saviour, deep with an eternal depth, He reserved for its communication the final, as it is the most beautiful, of all His parables.

They had left the upper room in Jerusalem. He

was on His way to the garden of Gethsemane. A few moments before, He had communicated them. Never during all the days He had spent with them did He seem so near: mysterious intimacy bound them to Him. Then suddenly He stopped, as men will when something vital must be uttered, and in the silence of the night He said to them: *I am the true vine: you are the branches* .... *Abide in me*[1]. There was a time, which they could remember, when He had said to them: "He that eateth my flesh and drinketh my blood abideth in me: and I in him"[2]; and they had been mystified. Not long since, in the upper room, He had said: *Abide in me: and I in you;* and they had wondered at His meaning. But now, in an image, He was telling them the kind of intimacy He wanted of them; and they understood. Their union with Him was to be a living one, permanent and fructifying, so that in Him the Church, His Spouse, would be a vine whose branches would fill the earth of centuries, blossoming and flowering under every sky, and bearing fruit that would be sweet to the palate of God and man.

Of the many fruits of this mystic vine the choicest one is holiness of life and of this holiness there is no understanding until it is seen as a sharing in the holiness of our Lord, Jesus Christ. This is the theme of the following essay, in which Father Eugene Boylan, within

---

[1]*John*, xv, 5.
[2]*John*, vi, 57.

a narrow compass, examines the unity of Christ and
Christians. To this examination he brings not only
the rich experience of the Cistercian monk but that
theological learning that comes of contact with great
minds in the Christian past and present. It is matter
of common knowledge that, in recent years, theologians
have been occupied with the question of the Mystical
Body. The recent encyclical of His Holiness, Pope
Pius XII, will give new impetus to these studies. But
it is impossible to read the illuminating pages of Father
Boylan without realizing that, in his eager charity, he
is presenting, in accessible and attractive form, the basic
principles of a true Christian life.

One tremendous thought is awakened in the reader's
mind by the following study of the Mystical Body:
not only is the destiny of the Christian bound up with
Christ but the destiny of our Blessed Lord is mysteri-
ously bound up with that of Christians. In the eyes
of God, Christ and Christians are mystically one and
it is only to the extent that this unity is realized and
intensified on earth that the eternal purpose of God is
realized in time. Just as in life the Incarnate Word of
God built up, day by day, the living temple of His
own humanity, so by the power of the Spirit, communicated by grace, Christ is engaged in building up
the Mystic Body of the Church to the praise and glory
of the Father. Father Boylan is careful to explain that
this mystic unity of Christians with Christ is not in-

compatible with that distinctiveness of human personality, which must be held, but it is a salutary thought
to realize that of such vital import is the common destiny of Christ and Christians that the alternative, the
option which is no option, is life or death: *Behold I set
before you the way of life and the way of death.*[3]

FATHER JAMES, O.F.M.Cap.

St. Bonaventure's University Hostel, Cork.

---

[3]Jeremias, xxi, 8.

THE MYSTICAL BODY OF CHRIST AND THE SPIRITUAL LIFE

CHAPTER I

CHRIST THE VINE

EVERY good husbandman knows that the dead earth of itself can never bring forth living fruit without some suitable seed or specimen of the necessary species. If one wants to grow wheat, one must sow wheat; if one wishes to have grapes, one must plant a living vine. But once the right seed is sown, it can turn the dead earth and the inert air into living replicas of itself; the vine can transform the slime of the earth into the luscious grape. By living plants the earth and the air become the food of animals. Animals in their turn must come from animals, but once the parent stock are available, they can breed; and in the course of time, the vegetation of the earth can be transformed into the living animal flesh.

In the higher order this is also true. No man walked the earth until God created the first man and the first woman. But the human beings born from them have the power to take into themselves the dust of the earth made ready for them by the plants and the animals, and to fashion out of this matter, human bodies living with human life.

The world and all that is in the world were made for man. But man was made for God; and God was not satisfied to make man His servant; He sought also to make him His friend. Friendship calls for some sort of equality, and in order that man might know God and love God with the knowledge and love of friendship, God raised man above the limits of human nature to a superhuman state. In His mercy and goodness He gratuitously conferred on man a participation in His own divine nature, raising him to what is called the state of supernatural grace. By this grace, and by the gifts that God gives with it, man can share in a created way in the divine life and has the power to live divinely. So radical is the change, that God can love him with the love He bears towards Himself. With this marvelous equipment, man was called to find his final happiness in sharing the joy of God Himself for ever in heaven, and he was invited to merit this happiness by living a superhuman life, animated by a superhuman love of God, which life and love God had freely given him.

To bring about this plan, God sowed new seed on the earth. He created Adam and Eve to be the first parents of the human race and raised them up to a supernatural state in which they were participators in the divine nature. They were intended to transmit this divine life to their progeny and so to beget new friends for God. But God left them their freedom of choice, and made their condition dependent upon the observance of His commands. By disobeying God's precept they rejected His proposal and lost their share of the divine life—not only for themselves, but also for the whole human race.

The ruin involved in that calamity is beyond all description. Man's final happiness lay in a supernatural union with God, and by the fall, man lost all power to achieve that happiness. His "supernature" was gone, and even his ordinary human nature, inadequate as it was for a superhuman destiny, was further weakened by the effects of the catastrophe.

As a source of supernatural praise and love for God the world was once more void and empty—there were no beings therein who could give Him that friendship and love which were to be the fruit and harvest of His whole creation. Moreover, the human race owed His justice a reparation for the offense, which was altogether beyond its power to make. If God's justice were to be satisfied for the revolt against His infinite being, only an infinite divine person could make full reparation.

It was as if the wheat grower had seen all his seed destroyed, as if the husbandman had seen all his vines killed by the frost. The parent stock as to the supernatural life had destroyed itself. The world—as far as divine or supernatural friendship was concerned—was barren and sterile. Man could not satisfy for his sins. Man could not be united to God. But God is a good husbandman. In His wisdom and mercy, He deigned to sow new seed. *And the seed is the Word of God.*[1] The Second Person of the Blessed Trinity was to become man, to live and suffer and die for the human race, to atone for their sins, and as the new Adam, to restore the union of love and friendship between God and men. The whole history of Jesus Christ on earth—His birth, His life, His passion and His death—is the sowing of the new seed. The resurrection and the ascension are the beginning of the growth of that seed. The whole history of mankind, especially of Christian mankind, is the story of the vine which grows from that seed and which includes in itself all life and all salvation.

Our Lord Himself tells us: *I am the Resurrection and the Life.*[2] *I am the Way, the Truth, and the Life.*[3] *Abide in Me and I in you. As the branch cannot bear fruit of itself, unless it abide in the vine, so neither can you, unless you abide in Me. I am the Vine; you are the branches: he that abideth in Me, and I in him, the same beareth much fruit: for without Me you can do nothing.*[4]

We may use this metaphor of the vine to illustrate

---

[1]*Luke*, viii, 11.
[2]*John*, xi, 25.
[3]*John*, xiv, 6.
[4]*John*, xv, 4, 5.

God's plan of restoration, which is to *reestablish all things in Christ.*[5] Consider for a moment the development of a seed cast into the earth. For a time it lives on its own store of food, but eventually it becomes so completely changed by the development of a root and a shoot, that it may be said to have died to itself. But its roots gradually extend and penetrate all parts of the neighboring soil. Branching out in all directions, they seize upon the tiny particles of those materials in the soil, which are capable of being transformed into the substance of the growing plant. Under their action the dead contents of the soil are selected and transformed and made into the living matter of the plant, which is gradually pushing its way above the surface of the ground and sending out branches in all directions. The living vine, which is the final result of the process, and all its rich fruit, have been formed and fashioned out of the dead materials of the earth's clay and surrounding atmosphere, and yet there is a vital identity between the original seed and the ultimate tree. The life of the whole vine came from the life of the seed, but the material substance of the vine came from the surrounding earth and air. Plants then have the power of stretching out leaves and roots, of choosing a suitable material from their environment, of acting on that material, and assimilating it, making it part of their own self.

This process is a very good picture of what Christ

---

[5] *Ephesians*, i, 10.

does for the world. He resembles the seed sown in the earth—so closely, in fact, that He was buried in the tomb. Like the seed, too, He rises from the earth— *the first fruits of them that sleep.*[6] Every other soul who wishes to rise to eternal life must in some way become part of the Vine that is Christ, and share in the life that Christ gives us. *Neither is there salvation in any other. For there is no other name under heaven given to men whereby we must be saved.*[7] The rest of the organization of Christianity is merely a means of assimilating us into that Vine which is Christ. And the whole of the Christian life is "to abide in Christ." For Christ saves men by making them part of Himself.

God's plan for men involves the formation of some extraordinary unity, an organization, an organism, a body which embraces Christ and all who enter into life. The vine, of course, is only a metaphor—a figure of speech—and like all metaphors it must not be pressed too far or taken too literally. But that does not mean that the entity which it figures is not real. Quite the contrary, as we shall see. But the reality is so unique that we can only describe it by figures. And we may trace the parallel between the vine and that reality a little further. For just as the vine stretches out roots in all directions and seizes on the tiny particles of matter in the soil and changes them gradually into itself, so does the organization which our Lord depicts under

---

[6] *II. Corinthians*, xv, 20.
[7] *Acts*, iv, 12.

the metaphor of the vine reach out its roots to souls, offering them the chance of being incorporated into a newer and higher life, and of being transformed and made partakers in the divine nature. The formal entry into the Vine is made by baptism, but that is only the beginning. Complete unity and identification is the work of a lifetime; but unlike the development of the material vine, even the initial union with Christ involves the use of free will and deliberate choice in those who have come to the age of reason. That is one difference between the metaphor and the reality which is of capital importance for the spiritual life.

Another difference of even greater importance is that even when we have become part of the Mystic Vine by baptism, the continuation of our incorporation and, in fact, the closeness of our vital union with that Vine, unlike the fate of the material food of the natural vine, depend upon the continued exercise of our free choice and upon our cooperation with grace, which is the life-sap of the Vine. We shall consider these points in more detail in later chapters; at the moment we wish to draw attention to the general outline.

There is also another point in which the reality differs from the figure. In a natural plant, the original seed, as a seed, disappears; it grows into the whole plant and is no longer recognizable. In the Mystic Vine, the Seed is Christ, *the same for ever;* and, though it was by His death on the Cross that He merited life for us, He rose again for our justification,[8] becoming a quickening spirit for those who are united to Him. And Christ is intimately and personally present to each soul who is in the state of grace, and who is, therefore, a living branch of the Vine. His Body and Blood, His Soul and His Divinity, are intimately present to each soul who receives Him in Holy Communion. This intimate presence of Christ in each soul is something which calls for closer scrutiny. Here we draw attention to the fact that while the union between the different parts of the natural vine is limited by the laws of space and time, the union between Christ and His mystical branches transcends all limitations set by space and time. A thousand miles or a thousand years cannot separate or dissolve the intimate and vital union between them. Once united to Him by grace and love, only the will of the human "branch" can dissolve that union. The cleaving of our grace-aided will to God by love is the central point of our whole spiritual life.

This figure of the vine is rich in illustrations of the principles governing the spiritual life. Each tiny particle in the plant is "vine"; it is alive, it is in a supernatural state, it has the nature of the vine; but one could find evidence of the former nature it had before it was incorporated into the vine. This duality of nature runs through the whole spiritual life. The baptized soul has still a human nature with human defects and limita-

---

[8]*Romans*, iv, 25.

tions; but it has also a share in the divine nature and a share in the divine power of action, for it can perform supernatural actions. In particular it can bear supernatural fruit for itself and for others. Our Lord has stressed the fact that this fruitfulness is due to "abiding" in Him, for without Him "we can do nothing."

One notes in the vine, as in all organisms, a diversity of function in the different parts or members. Each cell is part of the vine, and yet not all have identical functions. So it is in the Mystic Vine; there is a diversity of function, as one sees in the hierarchy of the Church, and in the diversity of vocation in individual souls; yet each one in his own vocation is living the life of the Mystic Vine, and can only fulfill that vocation through union with the Vine.

Many more illustrations could be derived from the figure of the vine, but there are other figures which throw light upon this mystery. The principal one is that of the unity of the human body, which is used by St. Paul, and which we shall consider in the next chapter. Before closing this chapter, however, there is one illustration that might profitably be used to stress an important feature of the mystery which is not shown by the figure of the vine. In a vine, despite the vital identity of the seed, the root, and each member, there is no marked similarity between them. The whole vine is unlike the original seed; the branches, too, and the various parts show very definite differences. This is not quite true of the reality we are examining, for its structure can also be compared to that of a crystal. A large crystal can be grown from one tiny crystal of the same substance, by suspending it in a suitable solution of that substance. The crystals of each substance have a very definite characteristic shape. The original crystal, the final growth, and each component part of the final crystal, all have this characteristic form.

So it is with our union and unity in and with Christ. We must each resemble and reproduce the life of Christ in ourselves, and the final unity is not only like Christ, it is Christ—or, as St. Augustine expresses it, it is "the whole Christ." The principle of this unity is also the principle of the resemblance of the diverse parts, for this principle is the Spirit of Christ, the Holy Ghost, God Himself. As St. Cyril of Alexandria puts it: "Christ is formed in us by the Holy Ghost imparting to us a kind of divine form by sanctification and justification";[9] or again: "There is no union with God except by the participation of the Holy Ghost infusing into us the holiness of His own nature, and bringing us to His own life. . . . For the Son is the perfect image of the Father, and the Holy Ghost is the perfect semblance of the Son. Thus, transforming the souls of men to some extent into Himself, He impresses upon them a semblance of God."[10] St. Gregory writes:

[9] St. Cyril of Alexandria. *Ep. I ad Serapionem.* 24.
[10] St. Cyril of Alexandria. *Thesaurus Assert.* 34. Cf. *In Johannem,* xvii, 20.

"Christ with His whole Church, on heaven and on earth, is one single person. And as there is only one soul vivifying the different members of a human body, so the Holy Ghost vivifies and enlightens the whole Church."[11] The Church then is the Body of Christ, the Mystic Vine, the whole Christ. It is this figure of a body which St. Paul uses to illustrate our unity in Christ that we must discuss in the next chapter. But before closing this chapter let us try to visualize the whole process.

From all eternity, God knows Himself, and expresses His perfect knowledge of Himself in one thought, one word, Who is Himself God, the Second Person of the Blessed Trinity. Love follows knowledge, and from the Father and the Son, the knower and the knowledge, there proceeds a perfect love, Who is Himself God, the Holy Spirit, the Third Person of the Blessed Trinity.

In creating, God sees that His essence can be imitated or reflected in various limited ways outside of Himself, and decides to give existence to certain creatures who are made according to ideas in the mind of God. All these ideas are summed up in the one infinite Idea or Word who is God the Son, and in whom is found the exemplary cause of all that exists in creation. St. John tells us: *In the beginning was the Word, and*

---

[11]St. Gregory the Great, *In Ps. paenit.*, V. 1.

the Word was with God, and the Word was God. . . . All things were made by Him and without Him was made nothing that was made. In Him was life, and the life was the light of men.[12] St. Paul writes of the Son that He is *the image of the invisible God, the firstborn of every creature. For in Him were all things created in heaven and earth . . . all things were created by Him and in Him. And He is before all, and by Him all things consist. And He is the head of the Body, the Church, who is the beginning, the firstborn from the dead: that in all things He may hold the primacy. Because in Him it hath well pleased the Father that all fullness should dwell.*[13]

St. Thomas writes: "Since God, by knowing Himself, knows all other things, it follows that the Word conceived in God by the fact that He knows Himself is also one and the same 'word' of all things . . . though not in the same way. . . ." "All things, therefore, preexist in the Word of God before they exist in their own nature."[14] There is, then, even by mere creation, a relationship between the Word of God and all creatures. It must always be remembered that God does not get His knowledge from creatures, but rather by His knowledge creates them.

But God has gone further than creation. He has re-created men by making them participators in His

[12]*John,* i, 1-4.
[13]*Colossians,* i, 15-18.
[14]*Contra Gentiles,* iv, 13. Cf. iv, passim.

divine nature. To do this, He sent His Son, the Word of God, Who in some way sums up all things in Himself, into the world. Taking a human nature, the Son is the new Adam from whose fullness we are all to receive our new life. The Son sends His Holy Spirit into the soul of each Christian. When the Holy Spirit dwells therein He draws into the soul the Person of the Son, and the Son in turn draws the Father. It is by this indwelling of the Holy Spirit sent by the Son that we are made adopted—though real—sons of God.

The whole operation is breathtaking in its mystery and its magnificence. One point in its regard should be noted. We men love things because we see they are in some way good. But for God, things are good because and in so far as He loves them. The more He loves them, the more He conforms them to Himself. For us, too, our knowledge of things follows their existence. For God, things exist because He knows them.

Now the Holy Ghost is the love of God for God, proceeding from the Father and the Son. The Son is the figure of God's substance, and the perfect image of the Father. The more we are filled with the Holy Ghost and are subject to Him, the more do we reproduce Christ and the closer is our union with Him. It is to form the Mystical Body of Christ that the Holy Ghost is in the Church and in the souls of men.

CHAPTER II

THE BODY OF CHRIST

THE first metaphor we have considered in our discussion of this mysterious union of all baptized souls with and in Christ, is that of the vine. It is our Lord's own metaphor and it is especially suitable to indicate the origin of all supernatural life. Our Saviour Himself is the Seed and the Vine; we are now the "branches"; we were but the dead matter which the vine assimilated and vivified with life. This union which is presented under the figure of the vine must not be thought of as something vague, something shadowy, something figurative, something sentimental or fictitious. Indeed it is the greatest of all realities, for Christ is all in all, and the unity, as we shall see, is modeled on the unity of the Blessed Trinity itself. But the reality is so unique, so completely outside our everyday experience, so marvelous and so extraordinary, that we can only speak of it in metaphors. No metaphor can perfectly represent the reality, and, in fact—if taken too literally or pressed too far—any metaphor will only misrepresent the truth and mislead us.

Despite our divine Master's use of the vine, St. Paul did not hesitate to use another figure in his attempt to convince us of the wonders of incorporation in

Christ. It is true he speaks of our being "grafted in," as into an olive-tree, and he uses the marriage union of two in one flesh to illustrate the union of Christ and His Church; but his favorite metaphor is that of the human body. *You,* he writes, *are the body of Christ.*[1] St. Paul's choice of a metaphor in this matter is of the utmost significance. This mystery of our unity in Christ seems to have taken complete possession of his mind from the time of the famous revelation he received on the road to Damascus.

St. Paul, then known as Saul, and being as yet an unconverted Jew, was going down to Damascus to persecute the Christians dwelling there. He was struck down from his horse on the road and heard a voice rebuking him. *Saul, Saul, why persecutest thou Me?* To his inquiry: *Who art Thou, Lord?* he received the answer: *I am Jesus whom thou persecutest.*[2] This identification of Jesus with the members of His Church was the first revelation he received of the mystery of Christ, which is the dominant thought in all his writing. Filled with this idea and enlightened by further help from God, his constant effort was to bring home to us the reality of our incorporation into Christ, and he chooses as the figure for its expression the unity of the human body.

Let us examine for a moment what the unity of the

[1] *I Corinthians,* xii, 27.
[2] *Acts,* ix, 4, 5.

human body involves. In a human being we can distinguish a body and a soul. The body has many different members or organs, each of which has its own special function and relation to the benefit of the whole unit. We could carry the analysis much further, but for our purpose here it is sufficient to note that the whole structure of the human body is built up of tiny units which are called cells. There are living beings which are composed of a single cell; the human body contains millions of cells. In the body these cells are distinct living units, but they live with the life of the whole organism. The ultimate reason for that unity of life lies in the fact that all these tiny units are vivified by the same one principle of life—the human soul. It is on this account that they cooperate for the good and benefit of the whole. That, in fact, is the characteristic feature of organic life; diversity of structure with unity of life and purpose.

Some of these cells unite to form organs, each with its own function in the life of the whole unit; the eye, for example, is the organ of vision. But these different organs are interconnected by an intricate system of arteries, veins, glands, and nerves. They cooperate and assist one another, forming a single living unit, in which each organ operates for the good of the whole and not for its own benefit.

It is well to note that in the case of the human being a special perfection is found; for the human unit is a person. It is animated and vivified by a rational soul, having an intellect and will, as well as that type of "incommunicatibility" which is called subsistence.

St. Paul makes special use of the functions of the head to illustrate Christ's part in the life of the members. It is well to remember that in doing so, St. Paul follows the ideas of his time, and attributes to the head various functions which are now known to be exercised by other organs, particularly by the heart. He considers the head not only as ruling and coordinating the life and actions of the body, but also as giving it life through the vital circulation of the blood. In passing, we may note another peculiarity in St. Paul's usage on this point that must be understood. He sometimes speaks of Christ as the Head in distinction to the Body which is composed of His members, but he also speaks of Christ as the whole Body—including both head and members.

What may be said of the reality which St. Paul thus illustrates by the metaphor of a human body? That is a question which cannot be answered in one line or even in one whole book. Prat, in his exposition of the doctrine of St. Paul, gives a short statement of the mystery on which it is hard to improve: "Christ as Saviour associating every belief with His death and life."[3] Father Mersch, in his monumental work on the Mystical Body, formulates the mystery thus: "All of

---

[3] Cf. Prat, *The Theology of St. Paul*, II, p. 20.

us in Christ are one body, one man, one mystical
Christ."[4] St. Augustine expresses his view in various
ways: "All men are one man in Christ, and the unity
of Christians constitutes but one man."[5] "And this
man is all men and all are this man; for all are one since
Christ is one."[6] "When by faith, Christ begins to abide
in the inner man, and when by prayer He takes possession of the faithful soul, He becomes the whole
Christ, Head and Body, and of many He becomes one."[7]
"Our Lord Jesus Christ, like a whole and perfect man,
is head and body. . . . His body is the Church, not
simply the Church that is here in this particular place,
but both the Church that is here and the Church which
extends over the whole earth; not simply the Church
that is living today, but the whole race of saints, from
Abel down to all those who will ever be born and will
believe in Christ until the end of the world, for all
belong to one city. This city is the body of Christ.
. . . This is the whole Christ: Christ united with the
Church."[8] Two other expressions of St. Augustine,
used in reference to the prayers of the Church to which
the Psalmist refers as a "cry," are of capital importance: "Who is this man who reaches to the extremities
of the universe? He is one, but that one is unity. He
is one, not one in a single place, but the cry of this one

---

[4]Emile Mersch, *The Whole Christ*, p. 50.
[5]St. Augustine, *In Ps.* 39, En. 2.
[6]St. Augustine, *In Ps.* 127.
[7]St. Augustine, *In Ps.* 74.
[8]St. Augustine, *In Ps.* 90, *Serm.* 2.

man comes from the remotest ends of the earth. But how can this one man cry out from the ends of the earth, unless he be one in all?"[9] "This is but one man who reaches unto the end of time, and those that cry are always his members."[10]

Those quotations will give us some idea of the extraordinary unity that is expressed by St. Paul's figure of a human body. All those who believe in Christ, throughout all space and throughout all time, are united with Him and with each other as an organic vital unity in such a way that they form one mystical person. The unity is so unique that it is difficult to find a word to describe its nature. Some have thought of it as a moral unity. This is the type of unity found in those associa-tions of men who are united by a common end and purpose, to achieve which they submit to some au-thority. Such is the unity of national and domestic societies, of religious communities, and of the various political and economic organizations of men. The unity of the Mystical Body of Christ is something more than such moral unity. For this we have the authority of the Holy Father:

"Comparing the Mystical Body with a moral body, we must notice also between these a difference which is by no means slight, but on the contrary, of the highest importance. For in a moral body the only principle of unity is a common end, and a common aspiration of all

[9] St. Augustine, *In Ps.* 54.
[10] St. Augustine, *In Ps.* 85.

to that end by means of the social authority. But in the Mystical Body, with which we are concerned, there is in addition to this common aspiration, another internal principle, really existing and operative both in the whole structure and in each one of its parts, and this principle is of such surpassing excellence that by itself it immeasurably transcends all the bonds of unity by which any physical or moral body is knit together. It is something not of the natural, but of the supernatural order; indeed, in itself it is infinite and uncreated, namely, the Divine Spirit, who, in the words of the Angelic Doctor, 'numerically one and the same, fills and vivifies the whole Church.'[11]"[12]

The last sentence of this quotation from the Holy Father indicates a special feature of this union of all the faithful in and with Christ, which is splendidly illustrated by St. Paul's figure of the human body. For, as we saw, the unity of the human body is due to the fact that each member and each component is vivified and ruled by the same principle of life, the human soul. So, too, in this society of the faithful which we call the Mystical Body of Christ, the members are supernaturally vivified and ruled by the same principle of supernatural life—the Holy Ghost Himself, Who may be called the soul of the Mystical Body. We are only giving an outline here, but we again warn the reader that the metaphor of the soul, like that of the body, or

---

[11]St. Thomas, *De Veritate*, Q. 29, a. 4.
[12]Pius XII, Encyclical, *Mystici Corporis Christi*.

of "one man," must not be pressed too far. The human soul and the body form one single substance, each being in itself an incomplete substance. The Holy Ghost is the divine substance and cannot enter into a union with any creature so as to form one new substance. Nor do we human beings, in forming "one man" in Christ, cease to be individual persons.

If the unity of the Mystical Body is something more than moral unity, may one call it "physical" unity? The Holy Father discusses this question by comparing the Mystical Body with a physical body. He writes:

"Whereas in a physical body the principle of unity joins the parts together in such a way that each of them completely lacks a subsistence of its own, on the contrary in the Mystical Body the cohesive force, intimate though it is, unites the members with one another in such a way that each of them wholly retains his own personality.[13] A further difference is seen if we consider the mutual relation between the whole and each individual member; for in any living physical body the sole final purpose for which each and every individual member exists is for the benefit of the whole organism, whereas any social structure of human beings has for its ultimate purpose, in the order of utilitarian finality, the good of each and every member in as much as they are persons."[14]

---

[13]Note: Personality is used here in the technical sense of individual rational subsistence. It has not the popular meaning of characteristic temperament, behavior, taste, and outlook that belong to each individual.

[14]Pius XII, *loc cit.*

Therefore St. Paul's comparison of the faithful in Christ to members of the human body, must not be taken as indicating any interference with their personal identity or any denial of their own personal right and vocation to happiness. If they are incorporated in Christ, it is in order that they may share in His life and merits and attain to salvation and eternal happiness. But in doing so they give glory to God and to His Son. As the Holy Father writes: "For as the Church is fashioned for the benefit of the faithful, so is it destined for the glory of God and Jesus Christ whom He has sent." In this connection the pope condemns as false doctrine the view that "the divine Redeemer and the members of the Church are united to form one physical person, and consequently while attributing divine properties to human beings, they make Christ our Lord subject to error and human frailty. This false doctrine is as opposed to the Catholic faith and the teaching of the Fathers as it is repugnant to' the mind and the statement of the Apostle of the Nations, who, though he combines Christ and His Mystical Body in a marvelous union, yet contrasts the one with the other, as Bridegroom with Bride."[15]

Physical unity therefore does express something of the intimacy of the union between Christ and His members, but the comparison to the physical unity of the human body cannot be taken as indicating any loss of

---

[15]Pius XII, *loc cit.*

our personal identity in our union with Christ. Further, all such statements as those of St. Paul and St. Augustine, that we form "one man" in Christ, are to be read in the light of the Holy Father's authoritative interpretation of St. Paul, which excludes any idea of Christ and His members forming one *physical* person. That is why we speak of one *mystical* person formed of Christ and His members. This word brings out the uniqueness of the unity, but its reality is best expressed in Father Mersch's phrase as "ontological unity."[16]

The richness of meaning contained in these words will not be glimpsed until we have examined the nature of our life in Christ and His life in us in more detail. But lest the limitations that we have indicated in the use of ordinary words may have led the reader to imagine that this unity of man in and with Christ is something nebulous and unreal, let us point out that the most marvelous and most real of all unities is the unity of God Himself—in whom three distinct persons are united to form one divine being—and that our union in and with Christ is modeled on this union of the Blessed Trinity. This is evident from our Lord's Prayer at the Last Supper. For He prayed to the Father: *That they may be one, as we are One . . . I in them and Thou in Me, that they may be made perfect in one.*[17] And if we wish for a tangible proof of the intimacy of the union of ourselves with Christ, let us remember the

---

[16]Mersch, *op. cit.*
[17]*John*, xvii, 22-23.

sacrament of Holy Communion, and recall the words of Leo XIII. "The Eucharist, according to the testimony of the Holy Fathers, is to be considered as a continuation and an extension of the Incarnation. For through this sacrament the substance of the Incarnate Word is united with each individual man."[18]

The words used by Pope Pius XII must be read closely. He is speaking of the unity of the Mystical Body, and he says that it is something more than the unity of a moral body. He compares it with the unity of a physical body and shows where that comparison can mislead. He insists that the Mystical Body does not form one physical person, but to be strictly accurate, it must be said he does not discuss mere physical union as such, but is considering only the physical union of a human body. It is difficult to find words which are not liable to misinterpretation, not because of a lack of reality in the mystical union under consideration, but because of the unique nature and marvelous richness of that unity, which are such that they cannot be adequately expressed in ordinary words or accurately illustrated by ordinary examples. To form some idea of what this unity of Christ and ourselves involves, it is necessary to examine what effects it produces in us. Accordingly we shall examine how this union serves to heal the wound of sin in our souls.

---

[18]Leo XIII. Encyclical, *Mirae Charitatis*. May 28, 1902.

CHAPTER III

THE LIFE-GIVING DEATH

GOD'S plan to reestablish all things in Christ runs closely parallel to the course of man's ruin. Christ is the new Adam, and just as through Adam we received two things—our human natural life and the stain of original sin—so through Christ we are to receive the "reestablishment" of these two things—supernatural life and redemption. The metaphor of the vine is excellently calculated to show forth the former; the latter is more easily visualized by light of the comparison with the human body, though there are still many difficulties in forming a correct idea of it. There is a close connection between our revivification and our redemption; for the moment we shall consider the Redemption.

By the sin of Adam every member of the human race was deprived of that supernatural life and friendship with God which should have come to each one together with his natural life. Each of us is thus born stained by original sin. Although this sin involves no *act* of sin on the part of Adam's descendants, yet it implies that *state* of aversion from God and lack of supernatural love for Him which makes men displeasing in His eyes so that they are born children of wrath. To this original sin—the malice of which is beyond our

43

understanding—there are added the actual sins that every man commits in course of his lifetime. Sin, being an offense and rebellion against an infinite God, has something infinite in its malice. No adequate atonement for sin could be made to God's offended justice by a finite creature; only a divine Person could offer the infinite satisfaction that would be necessary if God's justice should be fully satisfied.

God, being both infinitely just and infinitely merciful, decided to exact complete satisfaction from the human race, but at the same time He deigned to provide humanity with an infinite Being to provide that satisfaction. The second Person of the Blessed Trinity became man and suffered and died in full atonement for the sins of His people. His very name, appointed for Him by God before His birth, shows the nature of His office: *He is to be called Jesus, which signifies Saviour; for He shall save His people from their sins.*[1]

Although every single act of our Lord's life was of infinite value, yet it was the will of God that the Redemption should be accomplished by His passion and death on the Cross. This death on the Cross was a sacrifice—a perfect, ritual sacrifice—*the* one sacrifice of which all other forms of sacrifice (save the Mass) are mere shadows and symbols—a sacrifice that gives God infinite honor and infinite glory, infinite praise and infinite thanks, infinite atonement and infinite satisfac-

[1] *Matthew,* i, 21.

tion—a sacrifice that is of infinite merit and is a perfect prayer.

Sacrifice is prayer in action. It is an action, a gesture, an offering, by which men profess their adoration, their love, their dependence, their desire, their submission, their gratitude to God. If their relations with God have been disturbed by the offense of sin, sacrifice will assume a new meaning of reparation and atonement, of appeasement and appeal for mercy. God's first commandment is that men worship Him. They are completely dependent on Him in every way. He is their creator, their ruler, their judge, and their final happiness. Without Him they could not begin to exist; without Him they could not continue to exist. In Him they live, move, and have their being; they cannot perform a single action without Him. The free and willing acknowledgment of all such relations with God constitutes worship. St. Thomas sums up our dependence in these words: "God is not only the cause and origin of our whole being, but our whole being is in His power and we owe to Him all that is in us." The most perfect public expression of this truth is the supreme act of worship called sacrifice.

This is not the place to discuss the history and the origin of sacrifice. In the Old Testament God had indicated the forms of sacrifice which He would accept. They foreshadowed the sacrifice of the Cross, and prepared men's minds for it. They generally involved the ritual offering by a competent priest of something belonging to men—usually something signifying life: living animals, food, or drink, for example—which was frequently destroyed or consumed in such a way as to express man's complete subjection to God.

The material sacrifice as such had no value for God. The external sacrifice was an expression of an internal sacrifice, and was only true and genuine when the interior dispositions it claimed to express were actually sincere and complete. This interior sacrifice can be summed up as a loving and willing acknowledgment that God is our beginning and final end; it offers Him, in adoration and in love, our entire self, all that we are and have, or may be or have in the future.[2] Without some such interior sentiments, sacrifice would be an "empty formula"—an open lie. Dr. Leen sums up the interior sacrifice as: "A filial and joyous conformity with the Divine Will, an aspiration after an ever more perfect union with Him, and gratitude for the pledges of that ultimate union already accorded."[3] In the case of the sinner, to these must be added an intention of propitiation and atonement. The more all these sentiments rule one's whole life, the truer will his sacrifice be and the more acceptable to God.

All these dispositions—even propitiation and atonement for the sins of men—are found perfectly in every

---

[2] Cf. *Summa Theologica*, II—II, 85, 2.
[3] E. Leen, *The True Vine and its Branches*.

moment of our Lord's life, from the very beginning, both in His Heart and in His actions. And in His sacrifice, since He Himself was the victim in whom all things are "summed up," they are most perfectly expressed. It was no mere coincidence that His very first utterance at the Incarnation was connected with sacrifice. We have St. Paul's citation of the prophet David as evidence of our Saviour's dispositions in that moment. Referring to the inadequacy of the sacrifices and holocausts of the old Law, the Apostle writes: *Wherefore when He cometh into the world, He saith:* '*Sacrifice and oblation Thou wouldst not, but a body Thou hast fitted to Me. Holocausts for sin did not please Thee. . . . Then said I: behold I come to do Thy Will, O God.*'[4] And the inspired writer adds words of extraordinary significance: *In the which will we are sanctified by the oblation of the Body of Jesus Christ once.*[5]

These dispositions then can be summed up as "giving glory to God by doing His will." The whole of Christ's life was lived in that disposition and is the result of it. All the actions and events of His life are as a rainbow of so many different colors into which the raindrops of the minutes break up the bright white sunlight of His loving zeal for His Father's glory expressed by submission to His will. These dispositions, which are the pith and core of His whole life, are

[4] *Hebrews*, x, 5, 6, 9.
[5] *Hebrews*, x, 10.

summed up and perfectly expressed in the sacrifice of the Cross.

To look at it in another way, let us recall the example of the seed which contains and "sums up" in itself the future tree. Suppose we imagine the process of growth and development to be reversed, so that the tree is condensed and "summarized" again in the seed. Then we should have some faint picture of how the sacrifice of the Cross sums up the whole life and dispositions of our Saviour. This comparison is offered because of its significance in connection with the sacramental system. The sacraments, especially the sacrament of the Eucharist, re-present and reproduce that seed in sacramental form and hand it over to us, so that we by our spiritual life have to make it grow once more in ourselves.

The comparison is undoubtedly farfetched, but it is not easy to find any adequate way of presenting these unique mysteries. As we shall explain, the Mass is a sacrament containing and "re-presenting" the sacrifice of Calvary, just as the sacred Host is a sacrament containing and "re-presenting" the Body of Christ. And St. Thomas shows that the Eucharistic sacrifice contains and "re-presents" all the spiritual realities of the Sacrifice of the Cross. "We do not say," he writes, "that Christ is daily crucified and killed, because both the acts of the Jews and punishment of Christ are transitory. *Yet those things which carry with them*

Christ's relations to God the Father, are said to be done daily (i.e., when Mass is offered): these are, to offer, to sacrifice, and the like."[6] On this point Father Brosnan writes: "The victim, by the manner of offering, now outwardly shows, and inwardly contains, all those things which carry with them Christ's relation to God the Father—that is, I take it, supreme worship, supreme love and obedience, superabundant satisfaction for sin, etc."[7]

The full significance of these words will become evident when we treat of the Mass. We cite them here to indicate the value of the sacrifice of the Cross. By it our Lord made complete atonement for sin. It is significant that in our discussion of sacrifice we found that atonement was by no means the most important part of sacrifice. This fact is reflected in the close connection between the Redemption and the restoration of supernatural life to the human race. But for the moment we wish to concentrate on the redemptive aspect of our Lord's sacrifice, for it will help us to come to some realization of the extraordinary intimate union that exists between Christ and ourselves.

Considering the double aspect of satisfaction and merit, at first sight there appears to be no great difficulty involved in this method of vicarious satisfaction and merit. Christ satisfied "instead" of us, He merited

---

[6]*In IV Sent.,* xii. In Lit.
[7]Joseph B. Brosnan, *The Sacrifice of the New Law,* p. 107.

"instead" of us! But on reflection one realizes that punishment and merit are personal things. The suffering or the reward may be transferred to another, but the actual personal stains of guilt, or the personal distinction and the pleasingness to God obtained by merit, seem to be inalienable.

St. Thomas states this problem in the form of an objection: "It belongs to him who has sinned to make satisfaction; but Christ did not sin: therefore He did not satisfy for *our* sins by His passion." To this objection, he answers: "The head and members are as one mystical person, and therefore Christ's satisfaction belongs to all the faithful as His members."[8] Elsewhere he writes: "The members and the Head are but one person. Therefore, since Christ is our Head by reason of His divinity and His superabundant fullness of grace, and since we are His members, His merit is not something outside us, but it is communicated to us or flows into us *(influit)* on account of the unity of the Mystical Body."[9]

The point is that there is here something more than substitution or even mere vicarious satisfaction. There is some principle of "solidarity" involved which results in a vital intimacy between Christ and His members. Instead of one person satisfying and meriting for another, it is rather as if one person was satisfying for himself. Two other quotations from St. Thomas will

---

[8]*Summa Theologica*, III, 48, 2, 1.
[9]*In* III *Sent.* d. 18. a. 6. sol. 1, 2.

illustrate the point. "The passion of Christ causes the remission of our sins by way of redemption. . . . The passion which He endured through charity is as it were a price; for by it, He, as Head, delivered us His members from our sins; just as a man by a meritorious work done by his hands, might redeem himself from a sin he had committed with his feet. For just as the natural body is one whole composed of many members, so the whole Church, which is the Mystical Body of Christ, is reckoned one person with its Head, who is Christ."[10]

Discussing the question whether Christ caused our salvation by way of *merit,* St. Thomas writes: "Grace was given to Christ not only as an individual, but as Head of the Church; that is to say, in order that it might flow from Him into His members. *Thus the actions of Christ have the same relation to Himself and to His members as the actions of a man in the state of grace have to the man himself.*"[11] No one who realizes the calm care with which St. Thomas chose his words can fail to realize the significance of these statements. If, then, we cannot find unions in everyday nature that are exact replicas of this union of Christ and His members, it is not because of its lack of reality. And if the Holy Father condemns as erroneous the idea of those who would have the individual members absorbed in Christ to form one physical person with the loss of

---

[10]*Summa Theologica,* III, 49, 1.
[11]*Summa Theologica,* III, 48, 1.

their own personal identity, it is because the unity of Christ and His members is in many ways something greater still, for it is union without annihilation. Despite all restrictions, we need not fear to conceive it as something close and intimate to an undreamt of degree, for by it all that is humanly His becomes ours.

There is a special feature of this union which begins at the time of our Lord's sacrifice on the Cross. There are a number of famous texts in St. Paul's epistles, in which the Apostle is forced to invent new words in his efforts to express our union with Christ in His passion, death, and resurrection. In the Latin, a number of words are used with the prefix "*con.*" The English translation is cumbersome and ineffective, and speaks of us as "suffering-together-with-Christ," being "crucified-together-with-Christ," "dying-together-with-Him," "buried-together-with-Him," "rising-together-with-Him from the dead," and other similar expressions. Father Prat's commentary on these texts is significant. "An examination of these curious words suggests three interesting observations: (1) our mystical union with Christ does not extend to the mortal life of Jesus; it originates only at the time of the Passion when Jesus Christ inaugurates His redemptive work; but from that moment it is continuous, and the *communicatio idiomatum* between Christians and Christ is henceforth complete; (2) that, if we go back to the source and origin of this union of identity, we see that it exists by right and potentially at the moment when the Saviour in the name and for the profit of guilty humanity dies for us and causes us to die with Him, but that it is realized, in fact and in deed, in every one of us, when faith and baptism graft us upon the dying Christ and make us participators in His Death; (3) that the author of it is none other than God Himself, Who, clothing us with the form and attributes of His Well-Beloved Son, recognizes us as children by adoption, and treats us thereafter as co-heirs with Jesus."[12] Elsewhere discussing the text, *Romans,* vi, 3-5, Father Prat writes: "In fact, we are associated with Christ and become His members just when He Himself becomes our Saviour. Now this moment, in the case of Jesus, coincides with that of His Death, symbolized and mystically realized for us in Baptism. From that time on we have everything in common with Jesus Christ; we are crucified, buried, and raised from the dead with Him; we share His death and His new life, His glory, His reign, and His heritage. Ineffable union compared by St. Paul to the grafting, which intimately mingles two lives even to the point of blending them, and absorbs into the life of the trunk the life of the grafted branch; a marvelous operation which makes both Christ and ourselves *symphytoi* (animated by the same vital principle), *symmorphoi* (subject to the same active principle), or, as St. Paul says elsewhere, clothes us with Christ and makes us live of His life."[13] In this connection let us

---

[12]Cf. Prat, *The Theology of St. Paul.* II. 19.
[13]*Ibid.,* I. 223.

quote St. Thomas: "The power of the passion is joined
to us by faith and by the sacraments."[14] "Baptism
incorporates us into the passion and death of Christ
. . . whence it follows that the passion of Christ in
which each baptized person shares is for each a remedy
as effective as if each one had himself suffered and
died."[15] "The baptized person shares in the penal value
of Christ's passion in as much as he is made a member
of Christ, as though he had himself endured the
penalty."[16]

Something more will be said in regard to the above-
mentioned limitation of our mystical union with Christ
to the moment of His death. But in view of the fact
that His death was the sacrifice which perfectly summed
up His whole life and dispositions, it is of great significance that our baptism, which is the summing up of
the life we are to lead, should be associated by St. Paul[17]
with that particular moment of His life. At the Last
Supper Christ had instituted that wonderful sacrament
of the Eucharist, which was to enshrine and give to
His members for all time, both Himself and His sacrifice. But the particular sacrament of baptism, by which
we become His members and are made capable of partaking of the Eucharist, is referred to the moment of
His death.

This moment is the center of all history; it is the

---

[14]*Summa Theologica*, III, 62, 6.
[15]*Summa Theologica*, III, 69, 2.
[16]*Ibid.*, ad 1.
[17]Cf. *Romans*, vi, 3.

focus and the center of all Christian life. In a sense, it stands in juxtaposition with every moment of history, and with every event of each man's life. One remembers how some maps of the world are drawn in Mercator's projection so that the North Pole, expanded into a line, is due north of every point on the surface of the globe. The sacramental system has something of this power of extending its pole or center; it "extends" Christ, and also Christ's sacrifice, so that He is in contact with every point of space and time. We have already quoted St. Augustine in regard to the idea of a mystical Christ extending throughout all space and time: "There is but one man, who reaches unto the end of time."[18] We would wish to remove the limitations of time sequence and space separation from the relations of the Head and members of the Mystical Body. For us, it is a four-dimensional entity, in which every part is in *immediate* contact with, at least, the Head. In fact, we would go further, and say that one can take any single moment or event in one's own life and place it in vital contact with any single moment or event in the human life of Christ.[19] And it would follow that every single event of Christ's life on earth must be considered as taking place in vital contact with each and every event in the lives of each and every member of His Mystical Body.

Of this vital contact we shall treat in the next

---

[18]St. Augustine. *In Ps.* 85.
[19]Cf. Eugene Boylan, *This Tremendous Lover.*

chapter. It is specially true of that outstanding event of His sacrificial death on the Cross. There we were one with Him. There He saw every single one of us and every single event in our lives. There He knew, in particular, every single sin of our lives, and made atonement for it, so that there is no sin which cannot be forgiven. This point is of capital importance. We can never exhaust the treasury of our Lord's satisfaction, nor come to the end of His mercy. It is not merely that He made a general provision for what might happen; He actually satisfied for every single sin we commit.

There is a deep mystery involved here. In some way, at least, by His knowledge, we were present and united to Him on Calvary, in His death and in His resurrection. We were at least as really present in Him and sharers in His actions as we were present in Adam and sharers in his guilt. But is that all? St. Paul writes: *Know you not that all we, who are baptized in Christ Jesus, are baptized in His death? For we are buried together with Him by baptism unto death, that as Christ is risen from the dead by the glory of the Father, so we also may walk in newness of life.*[20] Perhaps we may glimpse the full reality, if we take literally St. Paul's reference to the *Cross of our Lord Jesus Christ, whereby the world is crucified to me, and I to the world.*[21]

[20]Romans, vi, 3, 4.
[21]Galatians, vi, 14.

CHAPTER IV

IN CHRIST

JESUS Christ is the new Adam. The old Adam was "*a figure of Him who was to come.*" Christ is come that we may have life and have it more abundantly. St. Paul tells us: *But not as the offense, so also the gift. For if by the offense of one, many died; much more the grace of God, and the gift, by the grace of one man, Jesus Christ, hath abounded unto many. . . . For as by the disobedience of one man, many were made sinners; so also by the obedience of one, many shall be made just. . . . And where sin abounded, grace did more abound.*[1] Christ's obedience and His merit began at the moment of His conception. Any single one of His actions *could* have made adequate satisfaction for all sin, but God's wisdom decreed that the redemption should be accomplished by His passion and death.

On this point St. Thomas has an interesting comment: "From the beginning of His conception Christ merited for us eternal salvation. On our part, however, there were impediments whereby the effects of the preceding merits were debarred to us. For their removal,

---

[1]*Romans*, v, 15, 19, 20.

therefore, Christ must needs suffer. . . . The passion of
Christ had some effect that the preceding merits had
not, not because of greater charity, but because of its
nature, which was more suitable to such effect. This is
clear from the reasons given above concerning the con-
gruity of Christ's passion."[2]

This, perhaps, will throw some light on the special
nature of the mystical union between Christ and His
members in the final stage of His earthly life, to which
reference was made in the last chapter. It was not
until the obstacles to union were removed by the
sacrifice of Christ that the union of baptism became
possible; but once that was achieved, the time intervening between the sacrifice of Calvary and the particular
baptism of each individual soul does not count. The
two events must be placed in juxtaposition if we are to
obtain a proper picture of the relation. From that one
contact, two lives may be imagined as flowing in oppo-
site directions; the life of the Christian onwards and
the life of Christ backwards. But, although a new
union was produced at that great moment, we must
remember that even from the very beginning of His life
we were in some sense united to Christ.

Let us approach this general question of our union
with Christ from another point of view. Holiness is
certainly a personal perfection and achievement. Yet
our Lord at the Last Supper used these extraordinary
words in reference to the faithful: *For them do I*

---

[2]*Summa Theologica*, III, 48, 1, 2, and 3.

sanctify Myself that they may be sanctified in truth.[3]
On this text, St. Augustine makes the following
comment:

"But when He says: 'For them do I sanctify Myself,' what else can He mean but this: 'I sanctify them
in Myself *since truly they are Myself*'? For, as I have
remarked, they of whom He speaks are His members,
and the Head and Body are one Christ. . . . That He
signifies this unity is certain from the remainder of the
verse. For having said: 'For them do I sanctify Myself,' He immediately adds: 'In order that they too may
be sanctified in truth,' to show that He refers to the
holiness that we are to receive in Him. Now the words
'in truth' can only mean 'in Me,' since truth is the
Word who in the beginning was God.

"The Son of Man was Himself sacrificed in the
Word at the moment of His creation, when the Word
was made flesh, for Word and Man became one Person.
It was therefore in that instant that He sanctified
Himself as Man, in Himself as the Word.

"But now it is on behalf of His members that He
adds: 'and for them do I sanctify Myself.' That is
to say, that since they too are Myself, so they too may
profit by this sanctification just as I profited by it as
man without them. 'And for them do I sanctify
Myself,' that is, I sanctify them in Myself as Myself,
since in Me they too are Myself. 'In order that they

---

[3]*John*, xvii, 19.

also may be sanctified in truth.' What do the words 'they also' mean, if not that they may be sanctified as I am sanctified; that is to say 'in truth,' which is I Myself?"[4]

Elsewhere St. Augustine sums it up in one phrase: "Therefore *we too are He,* because we are His members, because we are His body, because He is our Head, because the whole Christ is Head and Body."[5] "*We are He,* since we are His Body and since He was made Man in order to be our Head."[6] "In this one Man, the whole church has been assumed by the Word."[7]

This notion of an "assumption" of all the faithful by our Saviour runs through the writings of many of the Fathers. Still more significant is the idea of a "summing up" of all the faithful in Christ, which is also frequent. St. Hilary writes: "Every man was in Christ Jesus, and so His body, the instrument of the Word, accomplished in itself the whole mystery of redemption."[8] "Thus, by reason of this body, all humanity is contained in Him. By this union of all men in Himself, He is like a city, and by our union with His flesh we are the inhabitants."[9] St. Cyril of Alexandria argues in the same way: "For the whole of humanity

---

[4] St. Augustine, *In Johannem,* 108.
[5] Sermon, 133.
[6] *In Johannem,* 109.
[7] *In Psalmum,* 3.
[8] *In Matthaeum,* ii, 5.
[9] *In Matthaeum,* iv, 12.

was in Christ as man,"[10] "For we are all in Him as man . . . . that He might destroy the law of sin which held sway in our members and also sanctify our nature."[11]

In St. Irenaeus we find a doctrine of "recapitulation of all men in Christ." This word, as Father Mersch points out,[12] "presents many meanings: a résumé, a taking-up of all since the beginning, a recommencement, a return to the source, restoration, reorganization and incorporation under one head. But these meanings are all related; in spite of their diversity, they fit into one another, and even when expressed singly, each one suggests the other." With this in mind, we can appreciate the significance of St. Irenaeus's words: "He *recapitulated* in Himself the long history of men, summing up and giving us salvation in order that we might receive again in Christ what we had lost in Adam, that is, the image and likeness of God."[13] And St. Augustine gives us a hint of the significance of the events of our Lord's life when he writes: "All that occurred on the Cross, at His burial, in His resurrection on the third day, in His ascent into heaven, and when He took His place at the right hand of the Father—all this happened in such a way as to prefigure, not in mysterious words only, *but*

---

[10]*In Johannem*, v, 2.
[11]*In Johannem*, x, 2.
[12]Emile Mersch, *The Whole Christ*, p. 230.
[13]*Adv. Haer.* IV. 38. 1. Cf. *ibid.* III. 18. 1.

in very reality, the Christian life that we are leading today."[14]

Leaving these statements of the Fathers for a moment, let us note that the doctrine of our association with the mysteries of Christ's life is used as the foundation for the teaching of one of the finest schools of spirituality we have: that, namely, which is founded in the writings of Berulle, Condren, Father Olier, and St. John Eudes. A more modern version of this principle is found in Dom Columbia Marmion's authoritative work, *Christ in His Mysteries.* He lays down as a fundamental truth that "the Mysteries of Jesus have this characteristic, that they are as much ours as His." He gives three reasons for this teaching. First, because Christ lived them for us. Secondly, because in all of them Christ shows Himself to us as our exemplar and model. Thirdly, because in His mysteries, Christ makes one with us. . . . "We make one with Christ in the Divine thought."[15] "God the Father unites the elect to His Divine Son in such a manner that all Christ's mysteries were lived by Him as Head of the Church. . . . Moreover all the graces He merited by each of His mysteries—He merited them in order to distribute them to us." And Dom Marmion sums up his doctrine: "Nothing is more certain than is this union of Christ with His chosen ones in the Divine thought; what makes Christ's mysteries ours is, above all, because

---

[14]*Enchiridion,* 53.
[15]Cf. *Ephesians,* i, 4.

the eternal Father saw us with His Son in each of the Mysteries lived by Christ and because Christ accomplished them as Head of the Church. I might even say that on account of this, *the mysteries of Christ Jesus are more our Mysteries than they are His.*"[16]

Father Mersch in his summing up of the teaching of St. Irenaeus writes: "Since by His very substance Christ is the source of grace, He is so always and in His every act. Whence follows the concept of the physical and mystical causality that all the events of His life exercise upon the sanctification of men."[17]

Even then if our mystical union through baptism with Christ has a special reference to the moment of His final sacrifice on Calvary, yet we can safely assert that our partnership with Him extends to every act of His life. The explanation of how this relationship is forged is a question we do not propose to discuss here; we merely wish to suggest some notions by which it can be represented well enough to give a sufficient grasp of it for practical purposes.

In the human body there is a mutual interaction between the different organs. The heart, for example, is affected by, and responds to, any strain or demand made on any other organ. But we cannot imagine the heart, today, being affected by tomorrow's strain, say, on the limbs in running! Yet we have to conceive such

---

[16]Marmion, *Christ in His Mysteries*, pp. 10-15.
[17]*The Whole Christ*, p. 24.

an interaction in the case of our Lord's relations with the members of His Mystical Body. He is affected and reacts to the need occasioned by every single sin of each of His members. He provides for every single grace each one needs to perform acts of virtue. And it is not a mere general provision. His life and death are perfectly fitted into those of His members. He is their perfect complement and their unfailing supplement in all things, "so that nothing is wanting to them in any grace."

To realize this, we have first of all to forget the time-sequence, both as to the interval and as to its direction. There is what one might call a "backward causality" in operation. For example, our Lady is conceived immaculate through the merit of Her Son's life and death some fifty years before He died. And we know how our Lord Himself suffered agony in Gethsemane on account of the sins and ingratitude of the present human race.[18] Just as a man standing on a hilltop can see the whole of a road between two points in one glance, so we must stand outside time and see Christ and His members as one complete whole, interacting on each other, despite their separation in time and space.

When we remember that every single action of any being, even of Christ, is completely subject to the will and providence of God the Father, and when we remember that the unifying principle of the whole

---

[18]Cf. Pius XI, Encyclical on reparation.

Christ, Head and members, is the Holy Ghost, whose action is qualified by His own eternity, for His life is *tota simul,* we may expect to find something more than mere temporal connections in the life of a Body controlled by Eternal Persons who always *are* God! If we think of God the Father as arranging every event in the life of His Son made man, to fit in perfectly with the actions of each of the faithful, perfectly known to Him at all "times," we shall not be far wrong. If we think of the Holy Spirit, harmonizing the actions of Christ with those of each of His members, again we may form some working picture of how perfectly Christ fits in with each of our needs. We must, at any rate, think of Christ as being affected by, and acting in view of, each and every event of each of our individual lives. In particular, we must regard Him as atoning in advance for each of our sins, and meriting for us each single grace that we need.

In fact, our Lord's life on earth was a perfect example of extreme and absolute altruism. He was God Himself, and He could therefore justly make Himself the end of all His actions. But instead, "He emptied Himself," and submitted Himself as man completely to the will of His Father and the guidance of the Holy Spirit. And while in all things He was doing the will of the Father in loving adoration, His whole life was also lived *for us.* In fact, one is tempted to say that He lived our life for each of us as it should be lived. The phrase could mislead, but it draws attention to the fact that through the merits and fruits of His life on earth, all the deficiencies of our own life can be repaired. He is our complement, our perfect supplement—*He is our all!* Gladly, then, may we glory in our infirmities that *the power of Christ may dwell in us.*[19]

To give a concrete picture of this vital connection between the mysteries of Christ's life and each moment of our own, which will not mislead, is not easy. Let us return for a moment to our picture of the seed developing into the tree, and the imaginary reversal of that process. Christ is a "summing up" of the whole of Christianity; that is clear from what we have quoted from the Fathers. The sacrifice of the Cross is the perfect "summing up" of Christ's relations with His Father, for it sums up His whole life. Now this sacrifice is contained "sacramentally" in the sacrament of the Eucharist, and, in fact, all the seven sacraments apply the passion and death of Christ to our souls. The first contact for each soul with the sacramental system is by baptism. Here one receives the life of Christ summed up as it were in a seed. The life of every Christian should be an unfolding and fulfilling of this seed and destiny given to him at baptism. This sacrament may be regarded as deleting all the space and time intervening between reception and the death of Christ. It puts the Christian in vital contact with the dying Christ.

---

[19] *II Corinthians,* xii, 9.

We have then the following time sequence. At the moment of the Incarnation our Saviour accepts the body "fitted" to Him, and embraces the full plan laid down by the Will of the Father: "A body Thou hast fitted to Me. Behold I come to do Thy will, O God." He is born and lives His hidden life and His public life in our name and in union with us. We might call this union mystical, but we must distinguish it from the closer union that is associated with His passion, death, and resurrection.

At the Last Supper, He institutes a sacrament—a sacred sign which contains Himself and His sacrifice. He then enters into the final stage of His life—His passion culminating in the actual sacrifice of Himself in a perfect oblation to the Father. On His side, at least, there is forged here a new link with us which closes on our side at baptism, which is the gate to the Eucharist. Father Prat, commenting on the text *Romans,* VI, 3-5, writes: "We are associated with Christ and become members of Him just when He Himself becomes our Saviour. Now this moment, in the case of Jesus, coincided with that of His death, symbolized and mystically realized for us at baptism. [Baptism then would seem to be the moment when *for us, on our part,* Jesus becomes our Saviour, and the two moments must be considered as in immediate contact.—Author] From that time on, we have everything in common with Jesus Christ; we are crucified, buried, and raised from the dead with Him; we share His death and His new life, His *new death,* glory, His reign, and His heritage."[20]

The significance of this conception will become clearer in the next chapter, where we shall examine the nature of the sacraments. Our own personal part in the work of our salvation commences with baptism and the Blessed Eucharist. (For the moment the sacramental system is taken as a unit.) By these sacraments, we are incorporated into Christ, and receive His grace, His strength, His help—His very self. We receive also His example, and, in fact, in some mysterious way, we are mystically conformed to His death and resurrection. He gives us both a plan and the means to carry it out. He is our model, and our partner. He is our wisdom and He is our strength.

It is in the Blessed Eucharist that this duality is most striking. For the Blessed Eucharist is both a sacrifice and a sacrament. As a sacrifice, it places at our disposal our Lord's own sacrifice to offer to God, and through the sacraments we are made capable of offering that very sacrifice sincerely, and worthily. As a sacrifice it gives us a perfect expression of our complete dedication to God through Jesus; and as a sacrament, it gives us Jesus Himself with all the dispositions of His "inner sacrifice," so that He may make us capable of living according to that complete dedication to God which His sacrifice expresses.

[20]Cf. Prat, *The Theology of St. Paul.* I, 223.

CHAPTER V

THE SACRAMENT OF THE PASSION OF CHRIST

LIKE many other features of the divine plan for our restoration in Christ, the sacraments are something quite unique; there is nothing like them to be found in all nature. They are signs, but they effect what they signify. They signify grace and they confer the grace they signify. For example, the sacrament of baptism signifies a cleansing and it actually does cleanse us from sin by giving us supernatural grace. It is true that in giving grace the sacrament is only an instrument in the hands of God; but it is a real cause. Theologians even say that the sacraments "contain" the grace they produce.

We are here concerned with the sacramental system as a vital link between the life-giving death of Christ on the Cross and our own souls. Nowhere is this more clearly evident than in the sacrament of the Eucharist. When the priest, speaking in the name of Christ through the power given to him by the sacrament of ordination, pronounces the words of consecration over the bread, these sacramental words effect what they signify and the substance of the bread becomes the Body of Christ. When the consecrated particle is eaten by the communicant, this reception effects what it signifies and Christ becomes the food and nourishment of the soul.

But that is not the end of the marvelous significa tion. When the celebrant at Mass signifies symbolically the sacrificial death of Christ, by consecrating the bread and wine separately with words which refer separately to the Body and to the Blood, the sacra mental action actually effects what it signifies, and the sacrifice of Christ is once more offered on the altar. This mystery needs some closer inspection.

Perhaps the best way to view it is to consider the Real Presence of our Lord under either sacred species. The very same Person, Jesus Christ, the Son of God, who as man walked on this earth for some thirty odd years on the eastern shores of the Mediterranean, more than nineteen hundred years ago, is today really, truly, and substantially present in the sacred host, with His Body and Blood, soul and divinity. That is a mystery, but it is also a fact which every Catholic accepts. There is, however, one most important difference between Christ's presence in Nazareth and His presence on our altars. In both cases, He is substantially present; but in Nazareth He is present by His own "accidents"— quantity, position, appearance, etc.; while on the altar He is present by means of the accidents of the bread. The substance of the bread is changed; the accidents— position, size, etc.—remain, and fix and indicate His "sacramental" position. This form of presence is unique, and may be called "sacramental"; but by it the subject is really, truly, and substantially present.

The Body of Christ is a living substance; the sacrifice of Christ was an event. Just as the Body of Christ was present in its normal way on Calvary and is today sacramentally present on our altars, so the sacrifice of the Cross—an event which took place on Calvary in the thirties of the first century—takes place, really, truly, and we may say "substantially," at the altar whenever Mass is said, but . . . . *sacramentally*. It is "located" in time and space by the "accidents" of another event, which signify it and contain it. Theologians generally regard the double consecration as the event which is essential for this sacramental re-production, re-presenting, re-presentation, of the original sacrifice of the Cross. The Mass then is the sacrifice of Calvary made sacramentally present for us and for our benefit.

St. Thomas sums it all up in a few words. "It (the Mass) is nothing else than the sacrifice which Christ Himself offered."[1] "The effect which the passion of Christ produced for the world, this sacrament produces in man."[2] "This sacrament is both a sacrifice and a sacrament. It is a sacrifice in as much as it is offered

[1] *Summa Theologica*, III, 22, 3, 2.
[2] *Ibid.*, III, 79, 1.

to God; it is a sacrament in so far as it is received by men. It has the effects of sacrifice in him who offers it or in those for whom it is offered."[3] And finally: "The Blessed Eucharist is the perfect sacrament of the Lord's passion, since it contains Christ Himself and His passion *(ipsum Christum passum)*."[4]

And it contains not only the exterior sacrifice of Christ but also His interior sacrifice. We have already quoted St. Thomas to show that it contains "those things which carry with them Christ's relations to God the Father" (p. 48). Father Brosnan's comment on this text is well worth quoting again: "The victim by the manner of offering now outwardly shows, and inwardly contains, all those things which carry with them Christ's relation to God the Father—that is, I take it, supreme worship, supreme love and obedience, superabundant satisfaction for sin, etc."[5] Elsewhere he writes: "It ought to be clear that Christ's human nature must always contain the constituents of the inner sacrifice of the Cross, and that as Christ's human will and intention are always in perfect harmony with the Divine will and the intention of the Second Person which changes not, so when Christ's human nature is offered in sacrifice, it will always contain the inner sacrifice of the Cross and the identical relations which that same victim and inner sacrifice bore to God on the Cross."[6] These relations

[3] *Summa Theologica*, III, 79, 5.
[4] *Summa Theologica*, III, 83, 5, 2.
[5] Joseph B. Brosnan, *The Sacrifice of the New Law*, p. 107.
[6] *Ibid.*, p. 113.

to God are the essential part of our Lord's life and death.

We may say then that Our Lord sums up Himself and His life and death in the sacrifice of the Cross. He then embodies this sacrifice, in all its substantial and essential fullness, in the sacrament of the Mass. In this sacrament He and all His riches are at our disposal; in the sacrifice of the Mass, He gives us His sacrifice that we may offer it to the Father; and in the communion of the Mass, He gives us His own Body and Blood to be the food and drink of our souls. To be nourished by food, one must first be alive; to partake of such divine food, one must first be born into a divine or supernatural life. And in the Mass the sacrifice precedes the communion. To make that sacrifice one's own, one must have some official status; one must have some title to it; in fact, one must have some connection or share with the priest who offers the sacrifice. All these preliminary qualifications are given to the soul by the sacrament of baptism. By this sacrament the soul is cleansed of original sin, incorporated in Christ, vivified by His Spirit, and made a partaker of the divine nature, thus becoming a true, though adopted, child of God, living with the life of divine grace and sharing in all the riches of Christ. This sacrament corresponds to a supernatural birth and it impresses an indelible character on the soul. St. Thomas considers this character to be a participation in the priesthood of Christ. This is of great importance in connection with the sacrifice of the Mass, for it is not without great significance that the sacrament which incorporates us into the Body of Christ, makes us also, in some degree, a sharer in His priesthood.

By this character, which makes us share in Christ's priesthood, we are, as St. Thomas says, "deputed for Christian worship."[7] Now, the whole work of Christ was to restore the proper and divinely-intended relations between God and man. This Christ did by His one sacrifice on the Cross. Everything is contained therein, and everything therein is contained in the Mass. And by baptism we are given an official competence to offer the Mass, and a real title by which that sacrifice becomes our own. We would almost dare to say that it is now "our" Body that is being offered— for we are members of that Body. But, sacrifice is an external expression of an interior sacrifice and "devotion" to God. In a word, when one offers sacrifice, one says something to God. If we, too, are offering sacrifice with the priest, must we not mean what we say? And since the sacrifice is prearranged for us, must we not mean what it says? Must not we, as living members of Christ, have in us the mind of Christ, those relations of love and submission which He had with His Father?

The words of St. Thomas, though primarily referring to the priest at the altar, have a general reference to all who receive communion: "Whoever offers a

---

[7] *Summa Theologica*, III, 63, 3, 2.

sacrifice ought to become a partaker in it, because the external sacrifice which is offered is a sign of the interior sacrifice by which one offers oneself to God. Hence by the fact that he partakes in the sacrifice (by communion) the offerer shows that he really shares in the interior sacrifice."[8] If more is needed, the encyclical of Pius XI on reparation[9] could be quoted at length. We content ourselves with these words: "We must then form together in the august sacrifice of the Blessed Eucharist, the act of immolation made by the priest, with that of the faithful, so that they, too, may offer themselves up as a *living sacrifice, holy and pleasing unto God.*[10] Therefore St. Cyprian dared to affirm that 'the sacrifice of Our Lord is not complete as far as our sanctification is concerned unless our offerings and sacrifices correspond to His Passion.'[11]"

To this we would add the authoritative words of our present Holy Father, Pius XII: "In the Eucharistic sacrifice . . . . the sacred ministers represent not only our Saviour but also the whole mystical Body and each of its members; in that sacrifice the faithful are associated in common prayer and supplication: and, through the hands of the priest whose voice alone renders the Immaculate Lamb present on the Altar, they themselves offer to the Eternal Father this most pleasing victim of praise and propitiation for the needs of the

[8]*Ibid.*, III, 83, 4.
[9]Pius XI, Encyclical, *Miserentissimus Deus.*
[10]*Romans*, xii, 1.
[11]Ep. 63. n. 381.

whole Church. And as the Divine Redeemer, when He was dying on the Cross, offered Himself as the Head of the whole human race to the Eternal Father, so in this 'clean oblation' (the Mass) He offers to the Heavenly Father not only Himself as the Head of the Church, but in Himself also His Mystical members, for He encloses them all—even the weak and frail among them—most lovingly in His Heart."[12]

This is the central point of the whole scheme of Christian restoration. The sacrifice of Christ is renewed sacramentally, so that we may fulfil and add to it *our* part as sharers not only in His external offering as a priest, but also in His interior sacrifice both as a priest and as a victim—for we offer with Him and with Him we are offered.

Let us try to summarize it all. Christ lived a perfect life for God and for us. He summed up that life in His interior sacrifice and He expressed that interior sacrifice as the perfect external sacrifice of the Cross. This sacrifice He makes over to us in the sacramental sacrifice of the Mass. We commenced our taking over of it by baptism. When we offer up with Him the external sacrifice in sacramental form at Mass we must try to conform our interior dispositions to His interior sacrifice (for we must mean what we say), and then we must try to conform our whole life to these dispositions. He sums up and folds up everything into

[12]Pius XII, Encyclical, *The Mystical Body of Christ.*

the Mass; we have to take over that "everything" and unfold it into our own whole life. That is the time sequence. The supernatural reality is something less limited, for by our very unfolding we live not so much after Christ as with Him.

This notion of an unfolding—a development of something condensed, of something summed up and handed over to us sacramentally—can be applied to baptism. For baptism, one might so put it, gives us both the germ or seed of the divine life in which we are to participate, and also the pattern of its develop-ment. The texts of St. Paul which speak of us being crucified together with Christ and buried together with Him so that we may rise together with Him, are of a deep and mysterious significance in this matter. The old ritual of baptism by complete immersion stressed the idea of baptism both as a burial and death of the old self and a renewal and resurrection to a newness of life produced by the Holy Spirit through the life-giving waters of the sacrament. But these signs effect what they signify, so that there is produced in us a death— or at least a dying—of the old man, and a birth of the "new creature" in Christ. Still more mysterious and significant is the connection with the death of Christ, for it is from His passion and death that the sacraments draw their power. In fact, by faith and by the sacra-ments, the passion of Christ is linked with us *(copulatur nobis)*, as St. Thomas describes it. For in some mys-terious way we died to ourselves with Christ on the

Cross. And to achieve the fullness of that death and the consequent resurrection to a newness of life, all that is needed is the continued action of our own will by which, renouncing our own life of self-love, we endorse that dedication of ourself to God, and accept the subsequent life of grace in which we live for God and not for ourself.

Know you not that as many of us were baptized into Christ Jesus, were baptized into His death. We were buried therefore with Him through this baptism unto death, that as Christ was raised from the dead through the glory of the Father, so we also should walk in newness of life. [13] *All you who were baptized into Christ, have put on Christ.* [14] *Buried with Him (Christ) in baptism, in whom you are risen again by the faith of the operation of God, who hath raised Him up from the dead. And you, when you were dead in your sins. . . . He hath quickened together with Him, forgiving all your offenses. . . . For you are dead and your life is hid with Christ in God. When Christ shall appear, who is your life, then you also shall appear with Him in glory.* [15]

If we remember that we are offered up to God in union with Christ in the sacramental renewal of His sacrifice on the Cross, we shall have some idea of what the dedication involved in our baptism should lead to.

---

[13]*Romans,* vi, 3-5.
[14]*Galatians,* iii, 27.
[15]*Colossians,* ii, 12; iii, 3, 4.

We have already been offered; it behooves us to fulfill this offering throughout the whole of our life. The fulfilling of this offering by living according to the mind of Christ—who came to do the will of the Father—is the whole plan of the spiritual life.

It is by no means easy to form clear ideas of the connection and relation between Christ's death and resurrection and our own, and it is still more difficult to write with any clarity of such a mysterious union. The laws of time and space, of before and after, of here and there, seem to be set at naught. In some mysterious way we are crucified in Christ, we die with Him, and we rise with Him. Then nothing is heard of us for nearly two thousand years, and in some spot, perhaps thousands of miles away from Calvary, we are born! And having been born into a natural life, we are baptized into the supernatural life of the Body of Christ. Yet at this moment the passion and death of Christ are applied to our souls, and we begin to enact a drama of death and newness of life that in some mysterious way has already been realized in our name by the death and resurrection of Christ!

It will be of great help if we can by a mental effort wipe out the remembrance of the time-interval, and place the two events side by side—the death of Christ, and our death to ourself in baptism and in the subsequent Christian mortification. In fact, as we said, we must draw our map on Mercator's projection, that is,

we should try to view things in such a way that just
as the North Pole is represented as being due north of
every point on the surface of the earth by prolonging
it out to one long line at the top of the map, so too
we put Christ—and in particular that event in the life
of Christ most concerned with our present need—
alongside of each moment in our own life, and His
action and ours can be regarded as simultaneous. The
sacramental system can be conceived as a prolongation
of Christ's life and death for this purpose, and in this
connection, the significance of daily Mass and daily
communion is easily noted. But whatever way we
represent it, we must view the whole plan as one of
union with Christ. How far this may be carried may
be glimpsed in these words of St. Augustine in reference to the Cross: "There are four features we can
note in every sacrifice: he to whom it is offered, he
by whom; what is offered, and for whom it is offered.
When the one and true Mediator reconciles us to God
by the sacrifice of peace, He remains one with Him to
whom it is offered, He makes one in Himself those for
whom it is offered, and the offerer and the offered are
one in Him."[16]

Few writers after St. Paul have such a definite conception as St. Augustine had of our unity in Christ,
as something transcending all space and time. May we
again cite his wonderful summary of it all: *And there
shall be one Christ loving Himself*. But even in reading

---

[16]St. Augustine, *De Trinitate*, iv, 14.

St. Augustine, it is only by taking different texts and using one to supplement and explain another, that we can even begin to grasp the depth of his conception. He sees a unity in Christ that defies presentation from any one point of view. If, for example, one regards it as a union and partnership of the present moment, one loses the idea of a unity extending back to Calvary and concentrated there. If, on the other hand, one views it as a long vital chain of growth and development, like a vine planted on Calvary and budding in our baptism, one is liable to miss the vital circulation that here and now unites all Christians with each other and with Christ. It is only by taking a number of cross sections in time and in space—if one may so speak—that the fullness of the plan is glimpsed.

But one thing may be stressed. In some way we were all united to Christ dying on the Cross. Even before the Cross it was in Christ that we were predestinated and chosen.[17] But our baptism unites us directly to Christ on the Cross. Did not our Lord Himself say that if He be lifted up, He would draw all things to Himself?

This is the climax of that extraordinary process by which, according to many of the Fathers, Christ assumed "all humanity and summed them up in Himself." Father Salet in his excellent article, *Le Christ, Notre Vie,*[18] draws attention to certain facts which may have

---

[17]Cf. *Ephesians,* i.
[18]Cf. *Nouvelle Revue Théologique.* 1935. p. 789.

significance in reference to our question. Writing of Christ's special function by which, as Father Salet says, "He is essentially always and everywhere 'Head,'" he points out: "The end of the Incarnation is not that there should be one more man among men, even though he be a perfect man, the God-Man: but rather that there should be constituted one God-man 'recapitulating' humanity. There is one man who lasts till the end of time. The Incarnate Word is not one man among humanity, but the man who carries humanity, not a unity in a multitude, but the unity of the multitude. We are, in fact, dealing with an individual man, but with one who is unity itself."

The reason why we stress this point so much is that it is essential to grasp the fact that the life which begins in us in baptism is an unbroken continuation of the life which was laid down for us on the Cross. Christ is the Head: we are His living members; there is surely continuity of life between head and members. That is the life to which we must whole-heartedly devote ourselves, if we would lead a truly supernatural and spiritual life. If one may use a commonplace illustration of a sublime truth, we should compare the mutual dependence of the life of Christ and the life of the Christian to the two parts of a hinge; the pivot, where the two halves join, represents the juxtaposition of the Crucifixion of Christ and the baptism of the Christian, which should be considered as simultaneous with each other, for time and space do not count where eternal relations are concerned; and the fact that the two halves of the hinge can be folded flat in full contact with one another illustrates the fact that the life of Christ and the life of the Christian are not only continuous but are also in full vital contact and should be lived side by side. But for each of us, individually, this life commences in baptism, which we shall now consider.

CHAPTER VI

NEW CREATURES IN CHRIST

OUR Lord Himself told us that He came that men might have life and have it more abundantly. He is the new Adam: it was by His passion and death on the Tree of the Cross in complete submission to the will of the Father that He destroyed the obstacles created by sin, and became for us a source of supernatural life. This life-giving passion and death is applied to us by faith and by the sacraments. Baptism is the sacrament of our birth into the supernatural life, for as our Lord Himself said, a man must be *born again of water and of the Holy Ghost* to enter into heaven.

Baptism incorporates us into the Body of Christ; by it we receive from God forgiveness of our sins, and a newness of life. We become what St. Paul called "a new creature." We become participators in the divine nature; our souls are elevated into a supernatural state by habitual grace; our faculties are enriched by the infusion of the virtues, faith, hope, and charity, with the moral virtues, and also the gifts of the Holy Ghost; for we need this endowment in order to perform the acts of our new supernatural life. By baptism, as we have seen, we participate in some way in Christ's priesthood; but so radical is the change produced in us that in some way also we are even made partakers in His Sonship, for we become true children of God. We are, it is true, only adopted children; but unlike legal adoption, which does not change nature, this divine adoption actually makes a corresponding change in our nature. Our souls even become the dwelling place of God, wherein the Holy Ghost resides as in a temple and acts as the principle of a new life for us, making us truly the sons of God.

In an early chapter we compared our Lord's death to the planting of a seed which ramified out in all directions and seized upon the particles in the soul and incorporated them in itself. The sacramental system might be compared to this ramifying process, and baptism to the act by which the root takes possession of the particle of soil. In all living organisms which transform the nature of their food into their own substance, the process of incorporation is complete when the vital principle of the organism completely "informs" or vivifies and dominates the nature of the transformed food. In the Mystical Body of Christ, the Holy Ghost corresponds to this vital principle or soul, and indeed the Holy Ghost is given to us in each of the sacraments. Union with Christ is complete when His Spirit vivifies and completely dominates the members. At baptism, this process of vivification and control by the Holy Spirit begins in the soul of the baptized.

There is, however, a very sharp difference between

the figure and the reality; and it is on this difference that the whole nature of the spiritual life depends. When a living organism takes possession of a food particle and makes it part of itself, the new part loses its own independent substance; but in the case of the Mystical Body, each new member retains his own personality, and dominion over his own actions. Even when incorporated into Christ and vivified by the Holy Spirit, the Christian can decide in each and every action whether that action is to belong to himself alone, or whether it is to belong to Christ and His Spirit. In fact it is in this connection that our notion of the Mystical Body as a four-dimensional entity is significant, for perfect union with Christ demands not only our incorporation in Him, but the continual handing over to Him of all the actions of our life—our four-dimensional self, so to speak: our body in three dimensions with all its future actions in the time dimension.

That is why we referred to the baptism as the beginning of the process of our vivification; for the process will not be complete until our death and eventual entry into heaven. Our whole life consists of a continued series of decisions, of free acts of choice. In each human act we have to decide whether it will be ours or whether it will be Christ's, and the work of uniting ourselves to Christ will not be complete until the last moment, with its last choice, of our life. In fact, our physical death might be regarded as the ultimate completion of that mystical death to ourselves and that rebirth in Christ, which began on the Cross, which was applied to us and accepted by us in Baptism and which should be developed in us by a life of Christian self-denial and mortification. Of Christ is written that *He emptied Himself . . . . and humbled Himself, becoming obedient unto death, even to the death of the Cross.*[1] And He Himself warned us that *if any man will come after Me, let Him deny himself and take up his cross, and follow Me.*[2]

The reason for this is simple; St. Paul puts it quite briefly: *For you are dead; and your life is hid with Christ in God.* We are members of Christ; our own life is doomed to death (even to the eternal death of hell if we renounce God); the life of the Mystical Christ is now ours and will bring us to a glorious life in heaven. But we are still living *persons*. Life is defined as self-movement, and a person is his own master. To live in Christ as His members, we must be moved by His Spirit;[3] but as living persons we must also act ourselves by moving ourselves. It is this need for harmony and cooperation between our own actions and the workings of the Holy Spirit that is at the root of all the principles and problems of the spiritual life.

There is then a continual need for activity on our part even as members of Christ. To act we must will;

---

[1] *Philippians,* ii, 7, 8.
[2] *Matthew,* xvi, 24.
[3] Cf. *Romans,* viii, 14.

to will we must have knowledge. But all these actions, all this knowledge, all this new life, in fact, is supernatural; we cannot even form an adequate image of the Mystical Body in which we must live as members. So that the knowledge which regulates our actions in that newness of life, and the volition by which we cleave to the source of that new life, must be supernatural. Hence the need for the supernatural, theological virtues of faith, hope, and charity. The fundamental and first virtue of these is faith: *The just man lives by faith,* writes St. Paul.[*] Since man is a rational being, his will must be directed by knowledge in his intellect before he can act. One can either see or believe. God is invisible, and even the God-man is only seen as man; His divinity is known by faith. So, too, the whole of our supernatural knowledge which directs our life in Christ is faith. In fact, His members are often called "the faithful." Faith is really a sharing in the divine knowledge, and the virtue which enables us to accept that participated truth and make it our own is divinely infused by God. The need of faith becomes especially evident when we consider that we have to abandon our own life and to rely absolutely on the life of the Mystical Body of Christ. We cannot see or perceive Christ or His Mystical Body, even though there is a sense in which the Church is visible. To live with Him and by Him and in Him, all our actions must be guided by faith.

---

[*]*Romans,* i, 17.

But faith alone is not sufficient. It gives us knowledge, but we must also have strength, for the actions dictated by faith are supernatural and therefore superhuman. For this strength we must rely on the divine goodness as well as for all the helps necessary for us to achieve our supernatural destiny. It is by the virtue of hope that we firmly expect this divine assistance. Even with hope, our equipment is not sufficient, for knowledge and the certainty of strength are empty and sterile things unless our will is able to make use of them. To do this we need the sublime virtue of charity, which enables us to love God and even to tend to unite ourselves and all our actions more and more to Him and so to become His completely. These three virtues are the fundamental virtues of the supernatural life and they are infused into our souls with supernatural grace when the Holy Spirit comes to us in baptism. It is by them that we are united to Christ and can live as His members. It is by them that we can say with St. Paul: *I live, now not I: but Christ liveth in me. . . . I live in the faith of the Son of God who loved me and delivered Himself for me.*[5]

These three theological virtues are concerned directly with God, but to live in union with God as members of the Body of Christ we need other virtues to enable us to supernaturalize and to regulate the actions required by the conditions of our human existence. These are the infused moral virtues which are

[5]*Galatians*, ii, 20.

also given to us in baptism, and of which the cardinal virtues are prudence, justice, temperance, and fortitude. But there is also a wonderful endowment bestowed on our souls known as the seven gifts of the Holy Ghost.

We must never forget that incorporation into Christ means incorporation into a Body in which the Holy Ghost acts as a vivifying principle, comparable in some ways to the action of the soul in the human body. In fact, our vital union with Christ is due to our sharing His Spirit. Full and perfect incorporation demands that in all our actions we should be absolutely subject to Him as to a vital principle. He must rule all our actions. The gifts are intended to make us pliable in His Hands, so that we are moved by Him without resistance or irresponsiveness on our part. As the spiritual life develops in depth and intensity, the effect of these gifts, which can well be compared to instincts in the natural order, become more and more marked and important. As Leo XIII writes: "These gifts are of such efficacy that they lead the just man to the highest degrees of sanctity."[6]

All these wonderful riches are given us that we may be enabled to live in accordance with the new nature which is ours by baptism. We have already referred to God's goodness in raising Adam to the supernatural state. We are raised to this state in baptism, and this state is usually known as the state of sanctifying grace.

---

[6]Leo XIII. Encyclical on the Holy Ghost.

The wonders of grace need a special book for their treatment. We shall not attempt to portray them here, and shall be content with St. Peter's affirmation that by grace we are made partakers of the divine nature and radically capable of living the life of the Mystical Christ. So deep and so real is the change produced by it in our souls that we are truly sons of God—partaking in some created way in Christ's sonship and even in His priesthood. The magnificence of our new state is best gauged from the fact that henceforth our food must be the Body and Blood of Christ Himself!

Nor is our contact with God limited to the reception of the Blessed Sacrament. For the Holy Ghost takes up His abode in our souls at the moment of baptism as the gift of God and dwells in us as in a temple. But it must not be thought that He is inactive there. As we saw, He must be the first principle of all our supernatural actions. He pours forth His grace into our hearts, illumines our minds, strengthens our wills, and assists our weakness. If one does not take the expression too literally, it could almost be said that He is the soul of our soul. He is in us and we are in Him. And just as a piece of cold metal placed in a fire soon partakes of the fiery glow and emits heat, so we are set on fire by His presence, for He is the love of God for God, the living flame of divine love, and our cold hearts are set aglow by the radiance and contact of His ardor. Not only is He in our souls, but He is truly *ours*. He is our life and strength and love in all that we would do for God. By His sevenfold gifts, we are made more pliable, and can cooperate more readily in the movements He initiates in our souls.

It is true that wherever the Holy Ghost is present the other two Divine Persons of the Blessed Trinity are present also, but certain operations are for special reasons attributed to individual Persons. The Son of God is also in our souls, making us share in His Sonship and His priesthood. This participation puts us immediately in a special relation with the Father, for we can truly say to Him speaking in our own name as well as that of Christ: "This is Thy beloved Son in whom Thou art well pleased: hear Thou Him!"; and whatsoever we ask of the Father in the name of Jesus Christ, that He will give us. By baptism then we acquire a new title to the paternal providence of God the Father. Whatever He does to us, is done to a member of the Body of His Son, and since God is a Father in all His actions, all He does to us or permits to happen to us, is set for our closer identification and incorporation with Christ. He will purge us of our old selves so that we may bring forth more fruit, by abiding still more intimately in the Mystic Vine. As long as we place no obstacle in His way, we may be confident that all things whatsoever, even the malice of men, will work no ultimate evil in our souls, but will even give us a new measure of union with Christ. The important point to remember is that our confidence in the con-tinual paternal protection and solicitude is based not on our own merits, but on our membership of His Son's Mystical Body, and His own goodness and mercy.

This divine indwelling in our souls would be a subject for a book in itself. God's action on our souls is so manifold that even a mere enumeration of His functions would be too long. He is there as our sov-ereign Lord and Master, as our divine lover and friend. He is there as our Father and our Spirit, our life and our light, He is there as our ally, our partner, our helper, He is there as our sanctifier and our Saviour— the list is endless. Each single title could be made the starting point of a plan of the spiritual life, and each one throws new light on God's goodness and interest in us, and on the intimacy and reality of our union with Christ. By baptism then God is in us, and we are in God, and are made Godlike.

The effects of baptism do not end there. By it we are admitted to the other sacraments. If we sin, we have a remedy in penance; if we are in danger of death, extreme unction will prepare us for our entry into heaven. But the greatest of all these sacramental privileges is our right to the Holy Eucharist. There are few effects of incorporation produced by baptism that could not also be attributed to the Blessed Eucharist. In fact, baptism seems to produce its incorporating effects, one might say, in view of the Blessed Eucharist.

But in the august Sacrament we have Our Lord Himself as the Pledge and the Achievement of our union with God. *He that eateth My Flesh and drinketh My Blood abideth in Me, and I in Him.*[7] The importance of this sacrament in the spiritual life is a subject for separate treatment; here we can only remind the reader of all we have said of the summing up of Jesus Christ and His life and death, His passion and His merits, and recall how everything is so summed up in the Host placed on the tongue of the communicant that one can exclaim in full truth, "My God and my all." For the Eucharistic Christ is indeed our all. Each time He comes to us in the sacrament, He comes as our perfect complement, and an adequate supplement for all our deficiencies. There is not a single failure in our life for which He does not bring us a more than ample reparation; there is not a single weakness in our self for which He does not offer us a remedy. Truly the baptized soul can exclaim with St. Paul: *Gladly will I glory in my infirmities, that the virtue of Christ may dwell in me.*[8]

The right to this divine food is but one aspect of the Eucharistic privilege given by baptism. As we have seen, the Blessed Eucharist is a sacrifice as well as a sacrament, and by baptism we acquire an official title to offer the Mass as our own sacrifice. Incorporated in Christ, all His merits and His sacrifice are at our

[7] *John*, vi, 57.
[8] II *Corinthians*, xii, 9.

disposal. Every single Mass that is offered in the Church is offered in our name, and by our dispositions, and in particular by our assistance at the sacrifice, we can make a new claim upon its fruits.

Baptism also gives us a participation in the prayers of the whole Church. We enter into the communion of saints and are officially members of the Church, for the Church is the Body of Christ. There is a mutual sharing of prayer, of satisfaction, and even of merit. The life of the whole Church is affected by our fervor, and we in turn live in spiritual dependence on the Church. Our incorporation in Christ means a union through Him with all the other members of His Body. We are united to our Lady, to all the saints in heaven, to all living members of the Church on earth, to the suffering members in purgatory. We can share in all their works and merits, for we are all one in Christ. In fact, no single soul on earth works independently of the other members of the Church, just as no member or organ of the human body can act without the other members. The vital circulation of grace depends upon the prayers and sufferings of many souls; the sacramental system is committed to the custody of the Church; and our instruction and guidance in the ways of the spiritual life is to be derived from fellow members of the Mystical Body of Christ.

Our incorporation, then, in Christ makes us indeed a new creature, with a new destiny and a new nature, with new powers and new privileges, with new strength and new assistance. It gives us a new relation with God and with men. Even the ordinary events of every-day life are charged with a new significance for us, for in all things we may see the hand of the Father working for the benefit of the Body of His Son. *To them that love God, all things work together for good.*[9] So wide is the application of this text that we may safely say that even the malice of men and of the demons will only lead to good for us, as long as we remain in the love of God and are united to Him by charity. St. Paul himself seems filled with this spirit of absolute trust and reliance on God, as will be seen in the very chapter from which we have just quoted. *We are predestined to be made conformable to the image of His Son. . . . If God be for us, who is against us? If* we need an intercessor, Christ is *at the right hand of God, Who also maketh intercession for us.* Our strength is in Him, for *in all these things we overcome, because of Him that hath loved us. . . . Who then shall separate us from the love of Christ?*[10] For by baptism we have Christ for our very own, and He is our hope and confidence, as St. Paul exclaims: *God that spareth not even His own Son, but delivered Him up for us all, how hath He not also, with Him, given all things?*[11]

---

[9]*Romans*, viii, 28.
[10]*Romans*, viii, *passim.*
[11]*Romans*, viii, 32.

CHAPTER VII

LIFE IN CHRIST

WE have now seen what was our original destiny, and how it was rejected by Adam. We have seen God's further offer to us of eternal life in the new Adam, Jesus Christ. We have caught a glimpse of God's plan to reestablish all things in Christ, and noted how, as a beginning of that plan, the Son of God became man and lived and suffered and died for us. We have found that He instituted a marvelous but mysterious sacramental system by which His life and ours are put in vital contact, how we are baptized into the death of Christ, and have become members of His Mystical Body, a continuation, as it were, of Christ Himself. We have seen how He summed up all things in Himself, and summed up His whole life and dispositions in the sacrifice of Calvary. This sacrifice He has made over to us in the sacrifice of the Mass as an adequate reparation for all our shortcomings and a perfect summary and expression of what our new life should be. How then are we to live that new life?

In the last chapter we glanced at the equipment given to each soul at its incorporation into Christ at baptism. There it acquired a new nature and new powers for its proper operations. The first and most fundamental of these powers is the infused virtue of faith. We may safely conclude then that the beginning and foundation of our spiritual life is faith. We must *believe,* we must live by faith.

It is of the utmost importance to realize this; for the whole spiritual life is a life of faith. Our prayers depend on our faith, our use of the sacraments depends on faith. We find guidance through faith in God's Church and in God's providence. The supernaturalizing of the ordinary actions of the day is completely dependent on faith, and it is by faith alone that we can find and retain a true standard of supernatural values. Neither the sensible devotion that is *felt,* nor the intellectual ideals that are seen, are the true soul of the spiritual life. Both can be of great help, but ultimately we must depend on faith and on the will to believe in God and in His goodness, because He is God. It is true that charity is the consummation of the spiritual life, and indeed the summing up of all our obligations. Did not our Lord Himself tell us: *Thou shalt love the Lord Thy God with thy whole heart and thy whole soul, and with thy whole mind, and with all thy strength, and thou shalt love thy neighbor as thyself?*[1] Yet love presupposes knowledge, and the supernatural knowledge which leads to supernatural love can only be based on faith. Since love then must influence every vital act of the supernatural life if it is to be performed in full union with Christ, we may say that

---

[1] *Mark,* xii, 30.

every action in the spiritual life involves an act of faith. Hence its capital importance.

Closely allied to faith is hope. Since our spiritual life is supernatural, the strength and the impulse for its actions cannot come from our nature; without God we can do nothing. We must then hope in God and not in ourselves; we must be confident that God in His goodness and mercy will deign to aid us and to enable us to live according to the faith He has given us. This leaning on God, which seems to sum up the idea of hope, is a necessary feature of every action in the spiritual life, so that hope, like faith, is of capital importance.

We have St. Paul's word for it, and his words are the words of God, that the greatest deed, the most heroic sacrifice, even the faith that moves mountains, is useless, vain, and profitless, unless we have charity. In fact, he even states that without charity, we *are* noth-ing.[2] St. John is equally insistent on the need for charity, and shows us the way to Divine union in the pregnant words: *God is charity: and he that abideth in charity, abideth in God and God in him.*[3]

Although faith is the foundation of our incorpora-tion in Christ, yet without charity we cannot share in the life of the Mystical Body. If we remember that the soul of that Body is the Holy Ghost—who is the

[2]Cf. I *Corinthians*, xiii, 2.
[3]I *John*, iv, 16.

love of God for God, the living flame of divine love—
and that for living membership of Christ it is essential
that we be animated and moved in our actions by
the soul of that Body, we can see the essential importance of charity. For our wills are free; God will
not force their free choice; but until our wills are
given to Him we do not completely belong to Him.
Now it is by love that we completely give our will to
God. Even the other virtues of faith and hope are dead
and without "form" if they are not animated by love.
This supernatural love must come from the Holy Spirit,
and He, who is Himself the love of God, must be the
animating principle of all our works.

It should be noted that each of the three theological
virtues, which each in its own way unites us with God
directly, involves the use of our will. The knowledge
got by faith is of course in the intellect, but belief is not
the result of an intellectual judgment where the clarity
of the evidence necessitates an assent, but an acceptance
of truth, not yet evident in itself, which is made by the
intellect under the command of the will. This is still
more true of hope, while the will's function is quite
evident in charity.

St. Paul sums up the work of the development of
the Mystical Body in these words: *By doing the truth
in charity, we may in all things grow up in Him Who
is the head . . . Christ.*[4] That indeed is a perfect sum-

---

[4]*Ephesians*, iv, 15.

mary of the Christian's life in Christ. For the truth presupposes faith, activity presupposes hope, and charity is the bond of perfection which ought to be in all our works.[5]

This is the focal point of our whole spiritual life. Everything must be done for love of God in union with Christ. All that is not born of that love is outside Christ and of little or no worth. And it is of utmost significance that it is the very same virtue which unites us to God, that unites us also to the members of Christ. *If any man say, I love God, and hateth his brother: he is a liar. For he that loveth not his brother, whom he seeth, how can he love God whom he seeth not? And this commandment we have from God that he who loveth God, love also his brother.*[6]

We quote this text here to draw attention to the close relation between love of God and love of our neighbor. It is the same one virtue of charity that is the principle of both loves, or rather of both ways of loving God. The reason is that our neighbor is Christ, for Christ is all and in all. We cannot separate the Head from the members in our love; we must love the whole Christ, or else fail to have a supernatural love even for our own self—for we, too, are Christ. The vivifying soul of the Mystical Body, who is the Holy Ghost, is the principle of our love both for God and for

[5]Cf. *Colossians*, iii, 14.
[6]I *John*, iv, 20, 21.

man, since we love all in and through Christ. So that
we cannot be truly influenced or animated by the soul
of the Mystical Body unless we love the whole Body.
Nor indeed can we be perfect members of such an
organism, unless we live for the whole Christ, and not
for ourselves. Cells of the human body which live for
themselves are but a cancer; members of the Mystical
Body who live for themselves are a cancer in Christ—
they are anti-Christ. That, briefly, is the foundation of
our duty of fraternal charity, which must never be
separated from our love of God—for there is but one
virtue of charity. But in addition to our obligations
towards our fellow members of the Mystical Body,
there is something even more fundamental which is
essential to our life in Christ. This is conformity to
the divine will. It was the first sentiment that we
know of in our Lord's human life: *Behold . . . I come
to do Thy Will, O God;*[7] it is His own summing up
of His life: *I always do the things that please Him,*[8]
and the Holy Spirit by the lips of St. Paul tells us of
our Lord: *He emptied Himself . . . and humbled Himself, becoming obedient unto death, even to the death
of the Cross.*[9]

The need for this conformity is evident from a
consideration of our membership of Christ. If we are
to be His members in truth, we must live by the Soul of

[7] *Hebrews*, x, 9.
[8] *John*, viii, 29.
[9] *Philippians*, ii, 8.

His Body, who is the Holy Spirit, and we must be subject to the law of the life of His Body, which is submission to the Head. Viewed either way, we can only be true members of Christ when we are doing the will of God.

In fact there is something productive, something almost creative, about such conformity to the will of God. The ruin of the human race by Adam came about through disobedience; its restoration in Christ is wrought by obedience. It was at the moment she submitted to the will of God that Mary became the Mother of Christ, and our Lord Himself saw in this submission to God's will something greater than the mere physical fact of her motherhood. He even said that one who does the will of God is brother and sister, and even His Mother![10] This point we shall consider in the chapter on our Lady.

True love of God is impossible without submission to His will. For love is the giving of one's will to God, and disobedience is the removal of it from Him. Our Lord Himself made this submission the test and touchstone of our love. *If you keep My commandments, you shall abide in My love.* And He immediately links this with the precept of charity: *This is My commandment, that you love one another as I have loved you.*[11] It is most significant that He laid down

---

[10]*Matthew*, xii, 50.
[11]*John*, xv, 10-12.

these two principles when treating of incorporation in Himself as the Vine, after having instituted the sacrament of love and incorporation at the Last Supper.

These are the two fundamentals of the spiritual life: to live by the will of God, and to live in an organic union with one's neighbor. But from the point of view of practice, there is something which may be regarded as even more fundamental, without which there can be no Christian life. This is humility.

The importance of humility arises from the sovereign nature of God. There is one thing God cannot give to man: He has given us Himself and He still is God; but, because He is God, He cannot give His glory to another. God's plan in restoring all things in Christ is to glorify Himself by His mercy. There is then no limit to what He will do for us in His mercy, as long as we do not detract from His glory by our pride. That is why, as God Himself tells us, He resists the proud and giveth grace to the humble. The enormity of our pride becomes still clearer when we remember that our only hope of salvation is by our incorporation into Christ, from Whom we derive literally everything. He is all and in all. If then we glory in our excellence or our works, we are rebelling against God's sovereign rights, and we deny the very attribute that He wishes to manifest in our redemption, namely, His mercy. *What hast thou that thou hast received? And if thou hast received why dost thou glory as if thou hast not received it?*[12] Everything we have is borrowed, and we are worse than fools if we glory in anything but in the goodness of God as manifested in His Mercy to us, and in the Cross of Jesus Christ. *Know you not that . . . the Holy Ghost is in you, Whom you have from God, and you are not your own? For you are bought with a great price. Glorify and bear God in your body.*[13]

The essential virtue of the supernatural life is charity, but in practice humility has a priority of its own. All our spiritual life comes from God; and since we are members of Christ, in giving us life, God is exercising His Fatherhood. This He will do always if there is no obstacle placed by us which brings a principle of His own divine nature into play to restrain His action. As Dom Marmion puts it, God is "pure Act" —He is always in Act—He is always being a Father.[14] The only thing that can really interfere with that fatherly action is our pride—for by pride we appropriate to ourselves His glory which He cannot give us without ceasing to be God. Therefore, if we are humble God will do the rest; for He intends to glorify Himself by His mercy to us in His Son. Humility then is *in practice* the one essential requirement for the growth of the spiritual life.

---

[12]*I Corinthians*, iv, 7.
[13]Cf. I *Corinthians*, vi, 19, 20.
[14]Columba Marmion, *Christ the Ideal of the Monk*, p. 375.

We may then sum up our idea of the fundamentals of our supernatural life in Christ in six points, namely: faith, hope, and love of God, conformity to the Divine will, charity for our neighbor, and humility of heart. These seem to be the essentials—the rest is but their development under individual circumstances. It is by these virtues that we continue the life of Christ on earth and live in close union with Him. He lives in us and we live in Him. He crowns in us His own gifts and it is He who enables us to merit.

In Christ we are to be one as He and the Father are one; that is His prayer.[15] Perhaps the following words of Father Salet may suggest some of the fundamental principles of this life in Christ. Reminding us of our profound union in and with Christ, despite the distinction of persons, he writes: "The doctrine of the Blessed Trinity can always remind us of this possibility, for it reveals to us the mystery of Love itself, the perfection of which consists in the fact that there are three 'I's' without there being a 'mine' and a 'thine.' The true obstacle to union is not the distinction of persons, but the opposition of egoisms. It is possible for us to continue Christ—it is possible that Christ act and suffer in us—on condition that those actions which are ours are good and attributable to Him, and that they be actually attributed to Him, for they really are His; and on condition that one does not refer one's

---

[15]Cf. *John*, xvi.

personal acts to one's own self to make them egoistic and one's very own—on condition that one only exists and asserts oneself to give oneself to Him."[16]

So far we have concentrated our attention on Christ Himself. We must not, however, forget that another Divine Person, the Holy Ghost, plays a part in our spiritual life. Our Lord Himself warned the Apostles before His departure that He would send them another Paraclete. We receive this Paraclete, the Holy Ghost, first of all in baptism, and if we wish to continue Christ, we must live by His Spirit.

For our Lord let Himself be led completely by the Spirit of God. Pope Leo XIII writes:[17] "By the operation of the Holy Spirit, not only was the conception of Christ accomplished, but also the sanctification of His Soul, which, in Holy Scripture, is called His *anointing. (Acts,* x, 38). Wherefore all His actions were *performed in the Holy Ghost,* and especially the sacrifice of Himself: *Christ, through the Holy Ghost, offered Himself without spot to God (Heb.,* ix, 14)."

Speaking of our reception of the Holy Spirit in baptism, the Pope continues: "In this sacrament . . . the Holy Spirit enters into the soul and makes it like to Himself. *That which is born of the Spirit, is spirit (John,* iii,6). . . . We have said that the Holy Ghost gives Himself: *The charity of God is poured forth in*

---

[16]G. Salet, *Le Christ, Notre Vie, Nouvelle Revue Théologique.* 82. 1935, p. 785.
[17]Pope Leo XIII, Encyclical on the Holy Ghost.

our hearts by the Holy Ghost Who is given to us
(Romans v, 5). For He not only brings to us His
Divine Gifts, but He is the Author of them and is Himself the Supreme Gift, Who, proceeding from the
mutual love of the Father and the Son, is justly believed
to be, and is called *Gift of God Most High.* . . .

"The same Spirit is called Holy, for He, the first
and supreme Love, moves souls and leads them to
sanctity, which ultimately consists in the love of God.
. . . Through the Gift which is the Holy Ghost, many
other special gifts are distributed among the members
of Christ. Among these gifts are those secret warnings
and invitations which, from time to time, are excited in
our minds by the inspiration of the Holy Ghost. Without these, there is no beginning of a good life, no
progress, no arriving at eternal salvation. . . .

"More than this, the just man, that is to say, he
who lives the life of Divine grace, and acts by the fitting
virtues as by means of faculties, has need of those seven
gifts which are properly attributed to the Holy Ghost.
By means of them the soul is furnished and strengthened
so as to be able to obey more easily and promptly His
voice and impulse. Wherefore these gifts are of such
efficacy that they lead the just man to the highest degree
of sanctity; and of such excellence that they continue to
exist even in Heaven though in a more perfect way.
By means of these gifts the soul is excited and en-
couraged to seek after and to attain the evangelical

beatitudes. . . . Lastly, there are those blessed fruits, enumerated by the Apostles *(Galatians,* v, 22) which the Spirit, even in this mortal life, produces and shows forth in the just; fruits filled with all sweetness and joy, inasmuch as they proceed from the Spirit, Who is in the Trinity the sweetness of both Father and Son, filling all creatures with infinite fullness and profusion (St. Aug. *de Trin.*, I, VI, c. 9)."

To this action in the soul of the Christian, we must add the external action of the Holy Ghost in each of the Sacraments, and through the teaching and the direction of the Church's ministers. He is, in fact, the soul of the Mystical Body, which is the Church, and He animates every act of Christian life.

Just as the human Body of Christ was conceived and formed by the power and operation of the Holy Ghost, so also, in a somewhat similar manner, is the Mystical Body. It is by the action of the Holy Spirit that we become, and live as, sons of God and members of Christ, in each of whom is continued the life and love of Jesus Christ on earth.

Examples are better than explanation. We have one incomparable example of a perfect member of Christ. Let us then consider her who is the Mother of God and the Mother of that Mystical Body of which she is the perfect member.

CHAPTER VIII

MOTHER OF THE WHOLE CHRIST

IF it be possible to formulate adequately in one single title our Lady's place in God's plan—and many sound authorities deny that possibility—it would be by saying that Mary is the Mother of the whole Christ. Perhaps it may be true that not all her functions and privileges can be derived from that one title, but we know of no other which is so nearly a complete expression of them all. Mary is the Mother of God; Mary is the Mother of Jesus; Mary is the Mother of every single Christian; Mary is your Mother and mine. But Christ is God; Jesus is Christ, the Head; you and I are the Body of Christ. In a word, then, Mary is the Mother of Christ—of the whole Christ.

Tradition has often drawn a parallel between the origin and fall of the human race and their rebirth and restoration. Although human generation implies two parents, the unique position of Adam in God's plan is shown by the special creation of Eve with a unique relation of dependence upon Adam. In the restoration, Adam is replaced by Jesus Christ, and the Blessed Virgin Mary is the new Eve. By nature a child of Adam, by grace Mary is absolutely dependent upon Christ. Even her Immaculate Conception, free from the stain of original sin, is due to the foreseen merits of her Son. There is no single function in which she is not absolutely dependent upon Him, in which, in fact, she does not act as a member of His Mystical Body. It is well to remember that even before she conceived the Child Jesus in her womb, she had already conceived Him in her soul, by faith, hope, and charity, by love, submission, and humility. And our Lord seems to regard this maternity as something greater than her natural motherhood.[1]

No other member is so intimately and so perfectly united to Christ in His Mystical Body. So close and so complete is the union that we find that Mary—in so far as it was possible for a creature of her sex—is said to have a share in almost all the functions of her Son. It is true that the exact determination of her share in the work of the Redemption is still a matter of discussion, but it is quite safe to say that there is a sense in which she can be truly called Co-Redemptrix. In fact, Pope Benedict XV writes: "*It may be truly said that with Christ she redeemed the world.*"[2] There is no need here to consider how some theologians distinguish between the winning of our Redemption and the application of its fruits to our souls. In so far as we are redeemed and have become members of Christ, we can truly regard her as having a participation in our Redemption by her Son.

---

[1] Cf. *Matthew*, xii, 50.
[2] *Inter Sodalicia.*

There is a wealth of testimony in recent papal documents to Mary's share in the work of her Son. Pope Pius X summed up the extent of her merit for us by saying: "Mary, made sharer *(ascita)* by Christ in the work of human salvation, merited for us *de congruo* what Christ merited *de condigno*."[3] In the same encyclical the pope writes: "From the communion of sorrows and of will between Christ and Mary, she merited to be the worthy Reparatrix of the world, and therefore the Dispensatrix of all those gifts which Jesus obtained for us by His Blood and Death." Her position as the Mediatrix of all graces has been confirmed by a Mass and an office; and the universality of her intercession is best indicated by the classic words of St. Bernard: "God wills that we should have all things through Mary." The liturgy gives her the title of Queen—*Regina et Domina*—and her royal power is always ready to help us. One could fill many pages with her prerogatives, but here we wish to stress principally two things: first, that all these wonderful privileges are completely derived from her Son and Head, Jesus Christ, and are really the flowering and the fruit of her perfect membership of His Mystical Body; secondly, that all this immense power is devoted to her Motherhood of men—to her Motherhood of the Whole Christ.

To derive Mary's office as Mother of the Mystical

---

[3] *Ad diem illum*. 1904.

Body of Christ from her membership of that same Body may seem to involve a contradiction. But, first of all, let us remember that Mary herself is the fruit of Christ's merits, and that she conceived His physical Body—in her obedience to the will of God—by the power and operation of the Holy Ghost, who is the soul of the Mystical Body. Secondly, we must remember that our Lord's ardent desire and longing is to give Himself to men that they may have life and have it more abundantly. The very same dispositions that make Him the Saviour of His Body and its "quickening spirit," when given to Mary make her the Mother of that Body. Pius X leaves us no room to minimize the reality of this maternity. Reminding us that the purpose of Mary's conception of Jesus was not merely that He should be made man, but that He might thereby become the Redeemer of men, the Pope continues:

"Wherefore in the same holy bosom of His most chaste Mother, Christ both took to Himself flesh and also united to Himself the spiritual Body formed by those who were to believe in Him. Hence Mary, bearing the Saviour in her womb, may be said to have begotten also all those whose life was contained in the life of the Saviour. Therefore, all we who are united to Christ and are members of His Body . . . have issued from the womb of Mary like a Body united to its Head. Hence, though in a spiritual and mystical way, we are all children of Mary and she is Mother of us all:

Mother, spiritual indeed, but truly and really Mother of the members of Christ—who we are."[4]

If we recall all that has been said in the earlier chapters of this book about God's plan to restore all things in Christ, to redeem and save men by gathering them into one Body, forming one mystical person in Christ—we can see how all Mary's different functions —Co-Redemptrix, Reparatrix, Mediatrix, Dispensatrix —are summed up in her function as Mother of the whole Christ.

And this function is a significant example of how the life and work of Christ in each of His members adapts itself and manifests itself according to the nature of that member. The work of Christ is to redeem men by making them part of Himself. That work in Mary manifests itself as a maternal work of bringing forth all men in Christ, and Christ in all men. That is her function as the principal member of the Body of Christ. Various attempts have been made to symbolize this function by comparing her role to that of some organ in the body, but none have been quite successful. The function of the heart in circulating the life-giving blood is perhaps the best. But in reality, she is so closely united to Jesus in all His works that no one organ can symbolize her. Christ is both Head and the whole Body; may we not say that Mary is the Heart and in some way the whole Body also? All that comes to each member from Christ comes through her.

_____

[4]Pius X, _Ad diem illum._ 1904.

Given this universal and magnificent function in the restoration of all things in Christ, her method of working and her characteristic practices are of the utmost significance. First of all she is praised for her faith: *Blessed art thou that hast believed, because those things shall be accomplished that were spoken to thee by the Lord.*[5] Hope is implied in this faith, and shines forth throughout her whole life. Love—who dare try to express the love of Mary for God? The official words of the liturgy may give us some faint idea of what that love was. She loved God more than all the saints and angels together!

And how do these depths of virtue find expression? First of all in Christian charity; for her consent to be the Mother of the Redeemer of mankind, with the acceptance of the suffering that involved for her, was probably the greatest act of fraternal charity ever performed by a creature until she herself renewed it under the Cross. And her visit to St. Elizabeth and solicitude for the hosts at Cana show that her charity did not disdain to descend to familiar details. Secondly, by obedience carried to the heights of abandonment. We see it in the consent by which she entered into the plan of the Redemption: *Behold the handmaid of the Lord, be it done to me according to Thy word.*[6] We hear in her one commandment—the only instruction given to men by her who was to be their spiritual

---

[5]*Luke*, i, 45.
[6]*Luke*, i, 38.

Mother: *Whatsoever He shall say to you, do ye.*[7] The will of God was the law of her life. And finally we cannot help recognizing her humility. The Magnificat is its inspired expression, and the Holy Ghost makes His Spouse give testimony to the very virtue that made her pleasing to Him: *He hath regarded the humility of His handmaid. . . . He that is mighty hath done great things to me.*[8] That is an example of perfect humility—full recognition of the great things God had done for her, together with a complete reference of them all to the goodness and mercy of God.

If one seeks for further characteristics of the life of this the greatest of God's saints, one's findings can well be summed up in the three words: "ordinary, obscure, and laborious." Any comment on the lesson of such a life would dull the brilliant clarity of its limpid eloquence.

Mary, then, is a perfect example of the life of membership of Christ. Her whole life is based on faith, hope, and charity; it manifests itself in fraternal charity, sublime obedience, and amazing humility. These virtues permeate the whole of her actions. All else is but the response of these to the demands of individual circum-stances, which elicit those actions that God desires.

Devotion to Mary, then, by imitation of her virtues, is true devotion to Christ. But we can even go further,

[7]*John,* ii, 5.
[8]*Luke,* i, 48.

for we can even share in her special vocation as the Mother of Christ. We have our Lord's word for it that by doing the will of God we become His Mother.[9] That is easily understood if we remember what has been written about the part played by obedience in uniting us to the Body of Christ; the perfect member is perfectly subject to the life principle of the whole Body, which lives according to the will of God. And fraternal charity and humility have a similar effect in bringing forth Christ in us, and us in Christ.

There is still another step. Mary's physical maternity is exercised by preparing the things of the earth as food, consuming them and first making them her own, and then fashioning from them the Body of her Son. There is a parallel in the spiritual maternity. The way of true devotion to our Lady as taught by Blessed Grignon de Montfort, which consists in giving ourselves, with all that we have or do, now or in the future, completely to Mary, is surely the most perfect cooperation with her spiritual maternity of the whole Christ. No discussion of that is here possible, but we quote the authority of Pius X: "Who has not learned that there is no more certain and more expeditious way of joining all men to Christ than through Mary? . . . Clearly there is no other way left for us than that we receive Christ from the hands of Mary."[10]

---

[9]*Matthew*, xii, 50.
[10]*Ad diem illum.*

To realize how far-reaching and how essential in God's plan is this association of Jesus and Mary, one has but to recall two significant passages at the beginning and the end of Scripture. The first is that in Genesis— where, after passing sentence on our first parents for their transgression, God consoled them by the promise of the Redemption. Addressing the devil, He said: *"I will put enmities between thee and the woman, and thy seed and her seed: She shall crush thy head, and thou shalt lie in wait for her heel."*[11] The second is in the Apocalypse: *"And a great sign appeared in heaven: A woman clothed with the sun, and the moon under her feet and on her head a crown of twelve stars. And being with child, she cried, travailing in birth, and was in pain to be delivered . . . and behold a great dragon stood before the woman who was ready to be delivered, that when she should be delivered, he might devour her Son. And she brought forth a man child, who was to rule all nations with an iron rod; and her Son was taken up to God and to His throne. . . . And the dragon was angry against the woman; and went to make war against the rest of her seed who keep the commandments of God and have the testimony of Jesus Christ."*[12]

There is no difficulty in seeing in the words of Genesis a reference to our Lady; and Pope Pius X applies the words of the Apocalypse to our Lady, who,

---

[11]*Genesis*, iii, 15.
[12]*Apocalypse*, xii, *passim*.

though blessed in heaven, is still laboring in a mysterious birth. "Whose birth?" asks the Holy Father, "clearly ours, who are still detained in exile and have yet to be brought forth to the perfect charity of God and eternal happiness."[13]

Mary then is the Mother of the whole Christ. We can share in her work by bringing forth Christ in our own souls by humble and loving obedience to the will of God. We can ensure our complete union with Christ by true devotion to Mary, by a complete consecration of all that we are or have to her that she may form us in Christ, and Christ in us. She is the Gate of Heaven, by whom we enter into Christ. She is the Mother of the whole Christ.

---

[13]Pius X, *Ad diem illum*.

CHAPTER IX

CONSUMMATUM IN UNUM

A FULL discussion of the connection between the spiritual life and the doctrine of the Mystical Body of Christ could fill many volumes. Limited as we are in this small work, we have preferred to expound the fundamental doctrine, and to leave the details of the spiritual life to the writers of other volumes in this series. Here we must end abruptly with a brief summary.

If we must choose a formula to summarize everything, it would be difficult to improve upon the words of St. Augustine: *"And there shall be one Christ loving Himself."*[1] The whole spiritual life is a life of love, and Christ is the lover, and Christ is the beloved. Christ in the husband loves Christ in the wife. Christ in the Head loves Himself in each of His members, and Christ in each member loves Christ in all the others. And Christ in the Head and in each member loves God with a love that comes from the Holy Spirit, Who is Himself the mutual Love of the Father and the Son. And since Christ is God, in Him God loves and is loved.

The very last words of our Lord's prayer at the Last

---

[1] *In Epist. ad Parthos.* P.L. 35, 2055.

Supper were an appeal *that the love wherewith Thou hast loved Me, may be in them, and I in them.*[2] As individuals, our part in the spiritual life consists in an "entering-in" to Christ, a "putting-on" of Christ, an untiring quest for an ever closer union with Christ. We are to continue Christ, we are to reproduce Christ, we are to be Christ. It is true that we never cease to be our own self; but the model that our Lord proposed for our unity is that of the Blessed Trinity itself,[3] and according to that model, we may say of our union with and in Christ, that although in it the distinction between the "He" and the "I" never disappears, yet the perfection of that union tends to remove all distinction of "His" and "mine."

All His is already ours; it only remains for us to make all that is ours truly belong to Him. That we do by faith, hope, and charity—charity in its twofold aspect; by generous acceptance of the Divine will and by complete abandonment to it, and, above all, by true humility. After our Lord Himself, our principal model in this is our Lady, who is also, as we have seen, a powerful agent in bringing about our union with Christ.

Since union with Christ involves living membership of a highly organized body, each one will have his own special function therein—his own personal vocation.

---

[2] *John*, xvii, 26.
[3] Cf. *John*, xvii.

In fulfilling this vocation, no matter how ordinary, how obscure, or how laborious it may be, each one can find full union with Christ, Who is filled with the riches of the Godhead, so that nothing is wanting to any of His members. He is our sufficiency.

If we remember how He insisted upon the need for this union, we shall realize that union with Him is more important than the actual work to which we are called. His words are full of significance: *Abide in Me. . . . He that abideth in Me and I in him, the same beareth much fruit.*[4] And although one might think that we should abide in Him in order that our actions should be fruitful, it would seem more correct to say that the chief fruit and purpose of our actions ought to be that we may abide in Him. He is the *one thing necessary.* He is our God, He is our all.

This union ought indeed be the primary purpose of all our actions, rather than any apostolic fruit they might produce. For love demands union, and ultimately it is love alone that counts. Without this love, or charity, as St. Paul calls it, not only do our works profit us nothing, but we *are* nothing.[5] And this love in us that demands union is itself the fruit of union, for it is poured forth in our hearts by the Spirit of God, who is the living flame of the divine love of God for God.

This same Holy Spirit so sets the Heart of Jesus on

[4]*John,* xv, 5.
[5]Cf. I *Corinthians,* xiii.

fire with love for His Father and zeal for His glory that the one life He lived on earth is not enough for Him.[6] He thirsts to take possession of our hearts and our souls—of our whole life and all our actions, in fact—in order that He may live again in us to love His Father and give Him glory. Our life is but a continuation of His. He has commenced everything for us.

There are different ways of regarding the development of this union. We can view it as the unfolding of the germ of the life of Christ in our own soul—as the growth of Jesus within us. He was born into our soul, so to speak, at baptism, and we have to nourish and foster that life by the use of the sacraments, by our acts of faith, hope, and charity, and by living in humble submission to the will of God. Did not He Himself tell us that by doing the will of His Father we become His *Mother*?[7] Here is a point of view that puts us in active union both with our Lord and our Lady. For our spiritual life then is not only the continuation of His own life, but it is also a continuation of the work of our Lady. We are thus offering the best possible cooperation to the new Adam and the new Eve, and by bringing forth Christ in our lives we are giving God the greatest possible glory in our power, for Christ is *the brightness of His glory and the figure of His substance*.[8]

---

[6]Cf. de Jaegher, S.J., *One with Jesus*.
[7]Cf. *Matthew*, xii, 50.
[8]*Hebrews*, i, 3.

Or we can envisage ourselves as members of Christ becoming more and more perfectly united to Him as we perform our actions in union with the Divine will which regulates the life of His Mystical Body, under the action of the Holy Spirit, to whose impulses we abandon ourselves in loving humility. From this point of view, it is perhaps easier to see our fellow members in their true light, and to recognize our duty of fraternal charity.

Whatever way we view our incorporation in Christ, the result is the same: we have to live the life of Christ under the action of the Holy Spirit, in union with the Head, by faith, hope, charity, humility, and complete submission to the will of the Father. These are the fundamental virtues of union. They will manifest themselves differently in each member according to his function and vocation in the Body of Christ. But the external actions to which they lead draw their real value from this interior life and union from which they proceed.

And that is a point of capital importance. There can be no true spiritual life, active or contemplative, without a sound and healthy interior life. And it is the interior life that matters. From some particular soul, God may not want any special activity; their interior life of prayer is sufficient. In other cases, His will demands great external works. Where that will is known, the acts of the interior life cannot be sincere unless the soul is zealous in attempting to carry out the works indicated for it. Each member has its own function, and healthy membership demands the generous discharge of that function. But all members, by their very nature, are called to a life of union with Christ, to an interior life.

This interior life of prayer is but a continuation of the prayer of Christ on earth. In fact, the whole spiritual life, interior and exterior, is but a giving of our members—our hands, our mouth, all our faculties and powers—to Jesus, that in us He may continue here on earth His life of adoration of the Father by doing His will with us and in us. But it is our hearts and minds that He especially desires, for with them He can find new instruments to express His love for the Father, and to sing in His honor the new canticle of praise which is Himself. The interior life, then, of prayer and union with God, is not a mere ornament of the spiritual life, or something unusual or extraordinary to which only a few specially chosen souls are called; it is the vocation of every single Christian, for which each one is adequately equipped by the graces of baptism and the other sacraments. In this, as in all else, our sufficiency is from God, and in Christ we have found an inexhaustible source of grace and strength and power. His prayer is ours, His Spirit is ours, and He prays in us and with us and for us.

But prayer is but a manifestation of our whole life,

and our life must correspond to the life of Christ. His life finds its perfect expression in the sacrifice of Calvary. This sacrifice becomes ours in the Mass, and there we have a perfect summing up and perfect expression of what our whole spiritual life ought to be. To the utterance thus made at Mass on our behalf, we must conform ourselves. The Mass says something to God on our behalf. If we are sincere we must mean what we say. Let us examine this sacrifice somewhat more closely.

Christ's sacrifice on Calvary had a twofold aspect. There was the exterior sacrifice, by which He gave ritual expression to His interior sacrifice. This interior sacrifice was the long act of adoration and submission to the will of God that was His whole Life. Both are contained sacramentally in the Mass. There we have all the "things that carry with them Christ's relation to the Father": His exterior sacrifice, His interior sacrifice, His supreme worship, His supreme obedience, His supreme love, and His superabundant satisfaction for our sins. The Mass, then, has an intrinsic value in the eyes of God quite independent of our participation in it, and quite apart from its symbolic role as the expression of our own interior sacrifice. And since we are members of Christ by baptism, and marked with the sacramental character which is partial participation in the priesthood of Christ, we can offer that sacrifice to God on our own behalf, and, as a propitiation for our sins, its value need have no limits.

But this sacrifice is also an expression of the interior dispositions—in fact, of the interior sacrifice—of the offerer: it expresses adoration, submission, obedience, and love. If the sacrifice is to be truly ours there must be something in our hearts to correspond to this external expression. The external expression is here determined for us by our Lord. Just as His life was in perfect concord with the external sacrifice of the Cross, so must our life be in perfect agreement with the sacrifice of the Mass. There in fact is the·plan of the whole Christian life.

We have already quoted the words of the Holy Father on the Mass, and we saw that we are offered in the Mass by Christ our High Priest to the heavenly Father. We cannot claim to be truly united to Christ unless we truly endorse, in our hearts, this offering of ourselves and fulfill that offering by a life of humble obedience to the will of God. We, too, must always do the things that are pleasing to the Father. We must, like Jesus, humble ourselves and empty ourselves, becoming obedient unto death—to the death to our self, that God has destined for us.

This, of course, means a life animated by faith, hope, and charity. It also means a life of humility. We offer God sacrifice to profess to Him our own nothingness and to acclaim Him as our all, to offer Him our adoration and our reverence. The sincerity of this protestation is only verified by constant humility of heart. To this humility we must add complete submission to the will of God.

Each day, then, in the life of a Catholic who would lead a spiritual life—who would, in fact, live as a true Catholic and member of Christ—should flow and develop from the offering our Lord makes of him every day in Mass. The duties of the day are the fulfilment of the promise made of loving service; the hardships of the day are the evidence of that generous submission. If this task seems to be above our strength, let us remember that we are not alone. God is with us. And it must never be forgotten that it is in the Mass that He gives us His own Body and Blood as our food—so that we may have *His* strength to live *His* life. He has promised that those who eat this Bread, *shall live by Him*.[9]

Not only has He given us Himself, but He has given us His Spirit—God, the Holy Ghost—as a permanent gift who dwells in our souls to animate and strengthen us and to make us capable of living divinely as members of Christ. In all things that the will of God demands, God the Holy Ghost is Himself our strength more than adequate for their performance. There is then nothing in God's plan of which we are incapable.

That is why we can so confidently offer ourselves to God in the Mass. For in doing the will of God we become the "meat" of Christ; we are "consecrated"

---

[9] *John*, vi, 58.

and transformed into His Body by the action of the Holy Spirit. Each time we do His will for love of Him we are born anew in Him, and He in us. We give ourselves to Him by doing His will instead of our own, and we find in that very act that He is given to us. By living the Mass we become more and more one with Christ.

That is our whole destiny—for Christ is all. We bring Him forth in ourselves, through faith, hope, and charity, by doing the will of God in humble submission. He is the fruit of our lives, and we need seek for no other. No more is needed of us, even by God. For Christ is His glory.

God made the world for His glory. We must live for that glory. We cannot give Him greater glory than by bringing forth Christ in our lives, by putting on Christ, by entering into Christ, for Christ it is through whom and with whom and in whom, in the unity of the Holy Spirit, is all the glory of God.

BIBLIOGRAPHY

Anger, Joseph, *The Doctrine of the Mystical Body*. Translated by John J. Burke. New York, Benziger Bros.

Boylan, M. Eugene, *This Tremendous Lover*. Westminster, Md., The Newman Bookshop, 1947.

Brosnan, Joseph B., *The Sacrifice of the New Law*. New York, Benziger, 1927.

Grimaud, Charles, *Only One Christ*. Translated by James Newcome. New York, Benziger, 1939.

Jaegher, Paul de, *One with Jesus*. Westminster, Md., The Newman Bookshop, 1946.

Leen, Edward, *The True Vine and Its Branches*. New York, Kenedy, 1938.

Marmion, Columba, *Christ in His Mysteries*. St. Louis, Herder, 1923.
Christ the Ideal of the Monk. St. Louis, Herder, 1926.
Christ the Life of the Soul. St. Louis, Herder, 1935.

Mersch, Emile, *The Whole Christ*. Translated by John M. Kelly. Milwaukee, Bruce, 1938.

Mura, Ernest, *Le Corps Mystique du Christ*. 2 vols. Paris, Blot, 1936-37.

Myers, Edward, *The Mystical Body of Christ*. New York, Macmillan, 1931.

Prat, Ferdinand, *The Theology of St. Paul*. 2 vols. Translated by John L. Stoddard. Westminster, Md., The Newman Bookshop, 1946.

Salet, G., "Le Christ Notre Vie" in *Nouvelle Revue Théologique*. LXII, 8:785-809. Sept.-Oct., 1935.

Sheen, Fulton J., *The Mystical Body of Christ*. New York, Sheed and Ward, 1935.